THE SAGE OF SAIGON

STEVE CREWS

Order this book online at www.trafford.com
or email orders@trafford.com

Most Trafford titles are also available
at major online book retailers.

© Copyright 2014 Steve Crews.

All rights reserved. No part of this publication may be reproduced,
stored in a retrieval system, or transmitted, in any form or by
any means, electronic, mechanical, photocopying, recording, or
otherwise, without the written prior permission of the author.

Printed in the United States of America.

ISBN: 978-1-4907-4210-6 (sc)
ISBN: 978-1-4907-4212-0 (hc)
ISBN: 978-1-4907-4211-3 (e)

Library of Congress Control Number: 2014912863

Because of the dynamic nature of the Internet, any web
addresses or links contained in this book may have changed
since publication and may no longer be valid. The views
expressed in this work are solely those of the author and do
not necessarily reflect the views of the publisher, and the
publisher hereby disclaims any responsibility for them.

Any people depicted in stock imagery provided by Thinkstock are
models, and such images are being used for illustrative purposes only.
Certain stock imagery © Thinkstock.

Trafford rev. 07/17/2014

 www.trafford.com
North America & international
toll-free: 1 888 232 4444 (USA & Canada)
fax: 812 355 4082

ALSO BY STEVE CREWS:

Surviving Bien Hoa

A Death In Korea
And the Search For Answers

SAGE: A wise man, scholar, authority,
       learned man, philosopher, intellectual

The journey of a thousand miles starts with
a single step.
                - Chinese proverb -

PROLOGUE

THE SILENT WAR

Saigon was attacked in 1859 by a joint Franco-Spanish naval expedition. Napoleon III sent Vice Admiral Charles Rigault de Genouilly to lead the military forces against those of Tu Duc, the Emperor of Vietnam. It was done to aid colonial expansion on the pretext of the anti-Christian policies set forth by Tu Duc.

The French first took control of the province of Cochin China in 1863. Within the next ten years they had taken control of two other regions, Tonkin and Annam. Eventually the French took over Laos and Cambodia and the entire area under their control became known as French Indochina.

A mountainous region of Southeast Asia known as the "Golden Triangle," stretching across the borders of Thailand, Burma and Laos, was transformed into the major site of opium poppy cultivation. At one time, that area supplied close to two-thirds of the world's supply of opium. The British and French introduced opium to Vietnamese society, though the British concentrated most of their drug business in China.

The establishment of French opium factories in Saigon and other cities, made France's monopoly on the drug one of its more lucrative colonial investments. There was a steady growth in the narcotics trade that continued into the twentieth century. At times, the French had to struggle against international crime organizations for control of the distribution of the drugs. Even after the French government left Indochina for good in 1954, the drug trade remained. Several thousand French citizens remained in the new country of South Vietnam as well.

During the first years of U.S. involvement in South Vietnam in the early 1960s, narcotics abuse among American soldiers remained a relatively minor problem. As time went on, the problem got much, much worse.

In the late 1960s and early '70s, usage of heroin, which is a derivative of opium, sky-rocketed. Heroin is a strongly physiologically addictive narcotic, more potent than morphine. At least twenty-five percent of U.S. troops in Vietnam had used opium or heroin by 1971. The low cost of the drugs, their availability, and low morale within U.S. military units had a lot to do with it.

Opium sold for as little as one dollar per injection or two dollars for a small "tar ball" of it that could be smoked. Morphine sold for as little as five dollars a vial. When asked if he was afraid of getting caught using drugs, one GI replied, "What are they going to do, send me to Vietnam?" In his opinion, any consequences would be better than serving another combat tour in this God-forsaken place.

Heroin and opium flowed into South Vietnam by various means. The Viet Cong brought it in by boat and over land. GIs returning from R & R in Bangkok brought some back with them and some American pilots smuggled the drugs into Vietnam by air.

The drug epidemic got so bad that by the end of 1971, approximately 20,500 GIs required treatment for serious drug abuse while less than 5,000 troops were treated in hospitals for combat wounds.

Because much of the opium trade was directed by South Vietnamese officials in high government positions, U.S. military efforts to stem the flow of drugs was greatly impeded. And if that wasn't bad enough, their efforts were also made more difficult by the complicity of some American government agencies in the opium trade.

The Central Intelligence Agency (CIA) had lent some of its planes to the anti-Communist Kuomintang for use in their heroin-trafficking business. That was done in order to maintain good relations with pro-South Vietnamese growers. The CIA found at least twenty opium refineries that produced an estimated 750 tons of opium a year within the "Golden Triangle." They did not put an end to either the production of, nor the distribution of the drugs.

Before the big crackdown on drugs began later in the war in Vietnam, the U.S. military command had ordered some Army Green Beret units to buy certain opium products in order to establish good relations with pro-South Vietnamese growers, just like the CIA had done. The American public was kept in the dark about these and many other questionable activities that took place in Southeast Asian countries during the war.

Besides opium and heroin, marijuana was another drug produced in large quantities in Southeast Asia. A survey done by Military Assistance Command Vietnam (MACV) showed that marijuana could be bought in almost every store in the city of Saigon. A GI in Da Nang could buy a marijuana cigarette for a dollar, but in Saigon, where the supply was more plentiful, it cost only ten cents.

The Defense Department also conducted a survey, and their results showed that between 1969 and 1971, almost sixty percent of U.S. troops were using marijuana on either an occasional or regular basis.

Then one day, an incident occurred that upset a lot of people, including the President of the United States. A U.S. Air Force Security Police drug-sniffing dog had alerted on a flag-draped metal casket inside of a C-141 Starlifter transport plane. The aircraft had departed Tan Son Nhut Air Base in Saigon, South Vietnam earlier that day, en route to Travis Air Force Base, California. It had stopped at Clark Air Base, Philippines to refuel and let a couple of passengers off. The casket was manifested to Travis Air Force Base.

The casket was taken off the plane and sent directly to the base mortuary, under an armed escort. The label attached to the casket was marked "UNVIEWABLE REMAINS." Many metal caskets with the same label had been flown out of Vietnam over the years.

After the casket was opened, it was discovered to not only contain the remains of a young white male Marine Lance Corporal but also, hidden beneath the zippered body bag, were several small bags of heroin.

Someone leaked the news about this discovery and soon afterwards, newspapers across the United States began to sensationalize this new and shocking drug-smuggling method. The story even made the nightly news on all the major TV networks.

When the Commander-In-Chief got the news about it, he went ballistic. He'd served in the Marine Corps himself during World War II.

To find out that a young Marine who'd been killed in combat had been disrespected by others in uniform and used as a hiding place for drugs being smuggled, just about drove him crazy with anger. "Once a Marine, always a Marine" was the way he felt and this incident with the deceased Marine made the President mad as hell.

In a meeting with the government's top narcotics official, the FBI, CIA, State Department and Secretary of Defense, he made it abundantly clear that something had to be done about the drug problem within the military establishment ASAP.

At a televised news conference the very next day, the President made a major policy speech about the drug abuse problem. Putting them on the spot, in a special message to Congress, he asked for an extra $150 million dollars for combating the problem.

A very secret and silent war was now about to begin. The funding for it had just been granted by Congress and a squeaky wheel was about to be greased.

CHAPTER 1

In Saigon, a new unit had just been formed within the organization known as MACV. It was a joint task force, designated the 1st SIU, Special Investigations Unit. The first part of its two-fold mission was to help combat the drug problem that was affecting U.S. military personnel in South Vietnam and other parts of Asia. That mission was at the direction of the Commander-In-Chief. The second part was to combat graft and corruption that some U.S. military members were engaged in, that undermined the integrity of U.S. forces in the country. The commander of MACV had added the second part of the mission because he felt that the existing military law enforcement agencies needed some help.
     The 1st SIU was composed of twenty-five men from different military and civilian branches of the federal government. The Air Force provided three officers from various OSI, Office of Special Investigations detachments. The Navy provided three officers from its NCIS, Naval Criminal Investigative Service. The Army provided three officers

from various CID, Criminal Investigation Detachments and the CIA, Central Intelligence Agency added three of its field agents to the mix.

The other thirteen members of this unique, one-of-a-kind organization were all members of the Army. They provided administrative, logistical, communications and transportation support. Unlike the officers, these thirteen enlisted men had been transferred from units already in Vietnam in order to provide a solid foundation of experienced people in their respective military occupational specialties who already knew how to get things done.

The 1st SIU's chain of command was short and simple. All assigned personnel worked for the commander of MACV. The officers of the unit were either lieutenants or captains, with at least one previous assignment in the same line of work. They were all volunteers for this special duty assignment and had received additional small arms training at Fort Leonard Wood, Missouri en route to Vietnam. There were no rookies in this small unit and there was no time for any on-the-job training.

They were provided with travel orders that gave them carte blanche authority to travel anywhere in South Vietnam on any type of aircraft or ground transportation, with a travel priority equal to a TAD/TDY. Their orders also instructed all U.S. military organizations to provide them with any assistance requested, in helping them accomplish their mission. Their orders authorized them to work and travel in civilian clothes and to carry a weapon, either concealed or openly displayed. Since the orders were signed by Lieutenant General Albert Christianson, the current MACV commander, they wouldn't run into any problems with U.S. military personnel.

Their large office was located on the second floor of the enormous MACV Headquarters building, at the opposite end of the hall that also housed the office of the Deputy Assistant Chief of Staff for Civil Operations-Rural Development Support, also known as CORDS. That organization was run by an Army general. He and the other top brass that worked in "Pentagon East" had no idea that the 1st SIU was in their building. Unlike all the other offices there, the entrance door to the SIU office had no sign on it. That was done to help them maintain a low profile and hopefully keep nosey people away. Outside of the unit itself, only the commander of MACV and his second-in-command knew about them.

Security was so tight about the existance of the 1st Special Investigations Unit that Peter Thomas, the CIA station chief in Saigon, didn't know anything about the three CIA field agents assigned to the new unit. He was living comfortably in the Duc Hotel, only a few blocks away from his office in the U.S. embassy.

Before leaving Washington, D.C. for Saigon, the agents had been briefed about their special assignment. They were to have no contact with other CIA agents in Vietnam, and that included agents of South Vietnam's Central Intelligence Agency. Information leaks had been a problem in Vietnam so every precaution was being taken to keep the new joint task force and their mission as secret as possible.

Melvin Grant, U.S. Ambassador to South Vietnam, was a good friend of Peter Thomas. Ambassador Grant was an enthusiastic supporter of the current president of South Vietnam.

He told the U.S. president that Trung Ho Quoch was the best man for the job and was dismissive of his short-comings and accusations of corruption. However, based on what the Saigon CIA station chief had told him, the Director of the CIA didn't have much faith in the ambassador's judgement in regards to the South Vietnamese president.

Therefore, he had to keep the station chief out of the loop on this occasion. It wasn't something that was normally done, but then, this whole new joint task force venture wasn't exactly normal either. When the ex-Marine president said, "Jump," the CIA Director asked, "How high?" If the boss wanted the ambassador and station chief in Saigon to be side-stepped and left in the dark, so be it.

The way the Paris Peace Talks were going and the U.S. troop withdrawals too, it might not matter what happened over there much longer, the CIA Director mused.

On the night of December 19, 1971, only a couple of weeks before the 1st SIU became a clandestine part of MACV, two 122mm Soviet-built rockets his Tan Son Nhut Air Base. One of the six-foot-long, one hundred pound rockets narrowly missed the Air America compound which housed the CIA-run operations right across the road from MACV HQ. Luckily, nobody was injured and damage was minimal. The two explosions had broken a few windows and rattled a few nerves, but that was about all the Viet Cong got for their efforts.

That same night and only eighteen miles away, five 122mm rockets hit Bien Hoa City and the big air base nearby. Coincidentally, the CIA Regional Headquarters in Bien Hoa was also narrowly missed. As in Saigon, the attack caused no casualties and very little damage.

News of the attacks was broadcast by the Armed Forces Radio and Television Service the next morning. The radio announcer who greeted listeners with, "Goooood morning, Vietnaaaaam!" had already rotated back to the States. The new announcer wasn't allowed to greet radio listeners that way, nor was he allowed to mention anything related to CIA facilities or personnel in his broadcasts.

As the members of the 1st SIU drank their coffee just before their first morning briefing following the attacks, they now had something new about the war to discuss. The sergeant in charge of the admin section contacted the MACV HQ office that compiled reports from locations around the country that had been attacked and then briefed everyone in the SIU.

He added his own thoughts to the basic information that he passed on to all the off-officers in the meeting that morning.

"I think the VC know all about the CIA locations around here," he stated with a smile, trying to add a little of his own sense of humor to the news.

From the lack of response from the coffee sippers, he realized it was too early in the morning for any attempts at humor directed towards the CIA men that were present.

Captain Greg Daniels, U.S. Army, was the senior member of the 1st SIU, based on time-in-grade, time-in-service and the amount of gray hair on his head, according to him. He stood facing the seated officers and CIA men. Some of them were now sipping their second cup of coffee already.

"Now, the moment we've all been waiting

for, the first assignments." He paused a moment while he glanced down at the paper in his hand in order to read the names and info.

"Navy Lieutenants Bob Kosinski and Daniel Ventnor. You two gentlemen get to fly up to Phu Bai and determine if anyone assigned to the graves registration unit there was in any way involved with the drugs found in the casket of the Marine lance corporal that made the evening news a couple of months ago."

Lieutenant Ventnor spoke up first. "That was the case begun at Clark Air Base, right? When the drug-sniffing dog was brought on the plane and alerted on it?"

"That's right. And because a Marine outfit at Phu Bai runs the graves registration unit there where the lance corporal was taken after he was killed, it was felt that our NCIS personnel would be the best choice of teams to look into it. Everyone will get copies of their orders right after the meeting. Any questions?"

"No, sir," the two Navy officers replied in unison.

Captain Daniels looked back at the paper in his hand again. "The next assignment goes to Army Lieutenant Jim Mahoney and Air Force Lieutenant Bill Fisher."

He glance up for a moment and noticed two people in the room looking around, trying to see who their partner was going to be. I'd probably be doing the same thing if I was in their place, he thought.

"You two gentlemen get to sleep in your own billets again, staying right here in Saigon for now. You'll be investigating corruption within the Army and Air Force Exchange Service, specifically, the clubs that AAFES is responsible for managing. If your investigation leads to other locations outside of Saigon, you're free to pursue it elsewhere, but begin here because of the numerous clubs in the area. In a way, you guys get to go bar-hopping and get paid for it," he quipped, with his own attempt at a little humor.

That resulted in some good-natured ribbing from some of the others.

"Any questions?"

"No, sir," came from two different sides of the office.

Daniels swiveled his stance to his right so he could reach the coffee cup he'd placed on the desk behind him. His coffee, with cream and sugar, was still slightly warm. He took another sip, still in need of caffeine.

"There are three gentlemen that have the task of hunting down the sources of drugs that GIs in Saigon are buying, using and sometimes selling. Agents John Brenner, Steven Mann and Cecil Decker. Any questions guys?"

"Nope."

"None."

"No, sir."

"OK then. Our next team has the most members. Because there are so many military aircraft arriving and departing Tan Son Nhut Air Base daily, we're assigning four people to the next assignment. Navy Lieutenant Joe Wagner, Army Captain Larry Johnson, Air Force Captains Wendell Robinson and Barry Westbrook. You four have the mission of going after the drug smugglers that are using U.S. military aircraft to do their dirty work. That's **U.S. military** aircraft only," he added, for extra emphasis.

Captain Westbrook asked, "Does that include those small twin-engine planes used by colonels and generals?"

"Excellent question, Captain Westbrook. Absolutely! If anyone gives you a hard time, tell them to complain to the commander of MACV. You're just following his orders. That should satisfy them. Just don't tell them what unit you're with, and that goes for anyone else who runs into a problem. We're all under the direct orders of the commander of MACV, Lieutenant General Albert Christianson. Any more questions?"

Seeing the majority of the heads were shaking "no" and no voices spoke up, Captain Daniels reminded everyone to get copies of their orders before leaving the office and said, "Starting tomorrow, the military members on all teams will be in civvies. That's all I have for now. Let's go to work."

Unfortunately for Captain Wendell Robinson, he had to leave Vietnam on short notice the very next night. The American Red Cross notified him that he had a family emergency that required his presence ASAP. He left aboard a colorful Braniff Airlines B-707 "freedom bird" that was filled with one hundred sixty-four other GIs that were excited to be headed back to "the world."

A decision was made shortly after his departure that he would be reassigned to an Air Force base close to his home. That was what the Air Force referred to as a compassionate reassignment. A replacement was then found to take his place in Saigon with the 1st SIU. That replacement was First Lieutenant Tom Ross, U.S. Air Force. The 25-year-old would be arriving within a week from his home in Oklahoma.

CHAPTER 2

Henri Ferrand stood at the large window in his office that was on the second floor of the old two-story office building. From where he stood, he had a good view as he watched one of his company's freighters being loaded at the Newport docks on the Saigon River. The Lady of the Seas was an old converted Liberty ship that was once used to transport American troops to England and France during World War II. Recently out of dry dock, she sported a new coat of paint. Now the freighter was plying the sea lanes between Marseilles, France and Saigon, South Vietnam.
A wide variety of goods made in Europe were shipped to Saigon, and scrap metal, most of it a by-product of the war in Vietnam, was shipped to France. What Henri didn't know was, how much of the scrap metal and smuggled drugs were being transferred to other ships far out at sea. Even in his position as the Saigon Branch Manager of the Gulf of Lion Shipping Company, named after the Gulf of Lion on the southern coast of France, he didn't know the details of every-

thing that was going on.

What he **did** know was that he wanted out of the situation he was in. His wife was already dead and he and his daughter would be too if he didn't continue to cooperate with the man who owned the company. He must think hard and figure out a way to protect his daughter, who meant everything to him. He was even willing to die trying.

This particular ship had a Panamanian registry. Its crew consisted mostly of South Koreans, with a few Philippinos, Vietnamese and Chinese in the mix. The stevedores, customs inspectors and truck drivers who delivered the materials to be shipped out were all Vietnamese. Henri and the ship's captain were the only Frenchmen here today.

The Americans working at the Newport docks at the Port of Saigon were further away from the Newport Bridge than he was. The Saigon River had a bend in it here and his company's ship was between the bend and the bridge. The Americans and their ships were on the other side of the bend and totally unaware that most of what was being loaded on the Lady of the Seas today had originated in their country not so long ago.

When the United States government provided the military services of South Vietnam with helicopters, planes, boats, tanks, artillery, munitions, etc., American taxpayers footed the bill. When empty brass artillery shells were removed from Vietnamese firebases and battlefields for disposal, tons of it ended up here, along with other military-related scrap metal such as destroyed jeeps, trucks, helicopters, and armored personnel carriers.

South Vietnamese government officials had long ago figured out a way to get rich from the clueless government that was spending millions of dollars each week helping them to remain free from Communism. It was just too easy to take advantage of their generosity. And so they did, in many different ways.

Henri picked up his 10 X 50-power binoculars from the small table nearby. He'd purchased them at the Dan Sinh Market in Cholon a couple of years ago. San Francisco has its Chinatown and Cholon was Saigon's Chinatown. Cholon means "big market" and there were a couple of very big markets there. Many ethnic Chinese had lived there for more than three hundred years.

He'd been amazed at the huge amounts and varieties of military equipment and weapons sold in the shops in that market. As far as he could tell, most of it had been manufactured in the United States. He let his mind drift back to that day and could see the piles of helmets, boots, field equipment, weapons and ammo as clearly as if he was standing there now. The market vendors were also selling things like U.S., Viet Cong, North Vietnamese and South Vietnamese military unit insignia patches, dog tags, Zippo lighters and web belts. He had to barter for several minutes with the vendor, who eventually sold him the binoculars at what he considered a reasonable price. Who knew what the black market prices would be like tomorrow?

Now thinking about the present, he focused his binoculars on Newport Bridge. It was up-river, only about a quarter of a mile away. He could clearly see the South Vietnamese Army guards standing atop their sandbagged gun emplacements at both ends of the bridge. They were all looking at the vehicles and foot traffic that crossed the bridge in large numbers every day. Their backs were to him and he could see the rifles that were slung over their shoulders.

He felt bad for them because they were standing out in the hot sun with the weight of their helmets and flack jackets adding to their misery. It was another sunny and hot January day with clear skies and only a slight breeze now and then to stir up the heavy humid air.

Moving his binoculars downward a tiny bit, Henri could just make out the barbed wire coils at the point where the bridge support columns entered the water. There were guards on both banks of the wide river watching the underside of the big bridge for anything that looked suspicious. Small gunboats patrolled this part of the river on a regular basis too. These were all measures taken to help keep the VC away from the bridge. They had already blasted it with explosives several times in the past but never damaging it enough to put it out of commission. One never knew when they might try it again. Who knows, maybe even today, Henri thought.

VC divers had also managed to severly damage a ship docked at Newport a couple of years ago. Henri knew that he didn't have to worry about any of his company's ships being damaged or sunk by the VC. The government officials who ran the scrap metal and drug smuggling operation paid them off. His boss had informed him of that fact.

A smile broke across his face as he thought about the audacity and ingenuity of these people, and at the greed that kept both sides from killing eachother all the time. But, unlike them, he wasn't doing the job of overseeing this shipping business in Saigon because of greed. No, he'd been promoted by his company years ago and transferred from their Vung Tau office on the east coast, to Saigon. It was after arriving here that he'd been blackmailed into becoming a part of one of the largest drug smuggling operations anywhere in the world.

Opium, heroin and marijuana made more money for this shipping company than all of the other things they shipped put together, many times over. Now he was constantly thinking of ways to get out of this predicament. If only I'd been able to remain in Vung Tau, he thought. Maybe this would not have happened. C'est la vie.

Something moving caught his attention to the left of the bridge and he refocused his thoughts and the binoculars, curious to see what it was. As he squinted his eyes while trying to get the lens to focus, he felt the pain of a headache coming on. This was his second one this week and not a normal thing for him. He'd lived his entire life so far with only a couple of headaches in fifty-six years and now he felt the beginning of a second one within a week starting to throb.

Ah, it's only the flag of bright yellow with red stripes, he told himself. The South Vietnamese national flag that flew from a tall flagpole over the Vietnamese Navy Headquarters on Hai Ba Trung Street had unfurled a few times in a short-lived breeze. Most of the time it hung limply in front of the building near the Saigon River. Well, he mused, at least I wasn't imagining things. But, sacre bleu! This damned headache!

Henri set his binoculars back down on the small wooden table by the window where he always left them and walked over to his desk. It was a large one, made of solid oak. It was older and heavier than he was. With a good polishing, it still shined just like a new one. It had been brought to this country from France, back when this place was called French Indochina. It was his favorite piece of furniture. He also liked the fact that it matched the color of the wall paneling in his office. With the long window curtains, paintings and floor lamps, the decor made him feel like he was back in France again.

He kept a bottle of aspirin in one of the top desk drawers. He walked across the creaky wood floor and got a cup of cold water from the small Japanese-made refrigerator that occupied one corner of the office, then sat down heavily in the old leather chair that came with the desk from his home country so many years ago.

He swallowed two aspirin down in a single long gulp and exhaled loudly. Then he leaned forward with his elbows on the desk and began massaging his forehead with both hands. If this headache returned in a few days, he planned on going to the French-run Grall Hospital in Saigon. What next, he asked himself as he closed his aching eyes. What next?

Loud knocking on his office door startled Henri from his quiet reverie. Before he could say anything, the owner of the company walked in.

"Bonjour, Henri!"

"Bonjour, Hao," Henri greeted, not happy at all with this unexpected visit.

Mang Binh Hao was not a big man in size, but he was very, very powerful. He was also very, very wealthy. He was born Chinese but Vietnamized his name, for reasons Henri never learned. He had several legitimate sources of income like the Phuoc Tuy Textile Company, the stevedoring company that hired all the dock workers at Newport and the shipping company that was only legitimate on the surface.

With the help of others, Hao also had several illegal sources of income. He'd become the second richest man in all of South Vietnam. The President of South Vietnam was the wealthiest. It didn't hurt that he was the brother-in-law of the President's wife, Ly Than Mai. He was married to her half-sister, Ling Thi Xuan.

Hao knew that Henri could speak Vietnamese reasonably well for a foreigner but he liked to greet him in French, mostly to show off his fluency in that language. However, when they spoke about business matters, he preferred English because he knew that most of the Vietnamese employed in this building were very limited in their speaking and comprehension of it.

Mang Binh Hao stood only five feet four in height and maybe weighed 120 pounds if you counted his expensive tailor-made suit, dress shoes and over-sized ego at the weigh-in.

Henri looked at Hao's dark brown hair, brown skin, brown eyes, the made-in-Hong Kong tailor-made dark brown suit, then the brown wingtip dress shoes and thought, oui, a real piece of dung in human form. He detested the man.

Hao took a seat in the old leather over-sized chair at the front side of Henri's desk. The mild-mannered businessman always had a big smile on his face. That caused his face to wrinkle so much that he looked like he was sixty years old instead of forty, at least in Henri's opinion anyway.

"To what do I owe the pleasure of this visit?" Henri asked, with a hint of sarcasm in his tone.

"Mon ami, I drop by to let you know I go with Lady of the Seas today. I meet some buyers at sea, do business. Then I go Hong Kong and Singapore, do more business." Hao looked across the desk at Henri to see if that bit of information would elicit some kind of reaction. He'd been known to say a few things from time to time just to impress people. That's just the way he was, always trying to

impress other people either by the way he flaunted his wealth or his language skills or some other way. Instead of a look of surprise or questioning, he saw only a pained look on Henri's face.
"Henri, you not look so well today. Are you not well?"
"It's just a bad headache, that's all."
He hoped that Hao would leave soon. He couldn't stand being around him. It wasn't just the odor of nuoc mam on his breath that made him feel that way. It was mostly because Hao was the SOB that had blackmailed him into becoming a part of the corrupt side of this shipping business.
"Don't worry about me. I'll be OK in a little while. I've already taken some aspirin."
He didn't dare ask Hao what kind of business he was doing that required him to travel to Hong Kong and Singapore. He hoped to find out sooner or later. The less Hao thought he knew about him, the better he felt about his chances of eventually finding a way out of this situation.
"When I return, we go over business records, yes?"
"Yes, fine."
"And how is Genevieve, your enfant cheri?"
"She is well. Thank you for asking."
Henri didn't want to talk about his half-French, half-Vietnamese daughter. Not to this low-life anyway.
Hao, still smiling as usual, looked at his expensive Cartier watch, then excused himself. It was time to board the ship for his next "business" trip.
Henri got up with him and escorted Hao as far as the front door of the building that served as the Saigon Branch of the Gulf of Lion Shipping Company. They exchanged a few

pleasantries and that was that.

He was so relieved to see Hao go. At least he wouldn't have to see him again for a couple of weeks, the evil bastard. And he wouldn't have to pretend to be friendly when he visited either. Henri thought of himself as an ami de cour, an insincere friend, only because he had to be. His daughter Genevieve's life as well as his own, depended on it.

Henri returned to his office and unlocked one of the desk drawers where he kept his hidden journals. His headache was starting to go away and he wanted to make an entry about Hao's trip before getting busy with other things he had to do today.

Ever since the day Hao told him about this smuggling business using the merchant ships belonging to the company Henri had worked for since 1947, he'd been keeping a journal. He didn't like being blackmailed, told that he and his family would be protected and kept safe if he went along with the business deals and that their lives **wouldn't** be protected and kept safe if he didn't participate.

Neither Hao nor anyone else ever explained exactly what might happen to him or his family if he didn't play along. They didn't have to. He'd been living in French Indochina, then South Vietnam, since 1947. He knew what **could** happen.

His original plan had been to keep a journal and record all the things that he discovered to be illegal within the company. He would also write the names of people and their role in the illegal activities. Then he'd turn the journal over to the South Vietnamese authorities and ask for their protection and assistance in leaving the country if necessary. He'd take his family to his boyhood home of Marseilles, France and never look back. But then, many South Vietnamese authorities ended up in his journal and caused him to change plans. How naive he'd been!

After a few years, especially after the influx of American military personnel and their civilian counterparts, his journal began to look more like an encyclopedia than a mere journal. In fact, he had to buy six journals to hold everything he'd discovered. He had decided to include information about people and corruption that went far beyond the business along the Newport docks. The only way to get revenge for being blackmailed, he felt, was to let the world know about the human rats that lived and thrived in Saigon. Maybe somebody would be able to do something about it some day. He hoped he could find that somebody.

He hadn't made all these discoveries of graft and corruption by himself. Several different people shared their knowledge of various aspects of this tangled web of greed and need for power with him, including Hao. He'd also overheard other people talking, without them realizing it.

Flipping through the pages of one of the thick green hard-cover journals, Henri came to a page with Mang Binh Hao's name written at the top. The information he'd been gathering on Hao over the past couple of years had filled up several pages. He wrote today's date and followed that with information about Hao's trip on Lady of the Seas: Going to Hong Kong and Singapore on business.

The false bottom he'd made in the large bottom drawer on the right-hand side of his old desk would keep the journals from being found in case someone managed to force open the locked drawer. The office supplies he placed over the false bottom covered his secret hiding place very well, he thought.

Still, he worried about them being discovered. He trusted no one at the moment.

The journal entries on Mang Binh Hao, brother-in-law of the wife of the President of South Vietnam and second richest man in the country, was adding up to an impressive dossier of illegal activities. He was known to have good connections with the wealthy Chinese businessmen in Cholon, of which there were many.

All one had to do was read Chinh Luan, the Vietnamese-language newspaper or The Saigon Post, where photos of him appeared a couple of times in that English-language newspaper. Hao was a publicity hound when it served his purposes. The good deeds he did in public, like making large cash donations to charitable organizations, were a good cover for what he did in private.

Henri once overheard a story about Hao while he was eating a meal at his favorite restaurant. Two Vietnamese men were at a table next to his at Givral Restaurant, built by the French in downtown Saigon in the late 1940s. It was well-known by the French community as having the best French cuisine in the whole of French Indochina. He especially liked the fact that it had a real old-school French bakery, known for a wide range of tasty baguettes, pastries and sandwiches. You could smell the baked goods from a block away. He blamed his weight of 200 pounds and his 44-inch waistline on all that delicious French food. Luckily, his 5-foot 10-inch frame evenly distributed it so even in middle age, he didn't look too overweight. Still, he'd have to cut back on how many chocolate eclairs he ate each week, his favorite indulgence.

As Henri sipped his after-dinner demitasse that evening back in the Fall of 1968, he overheard a story that ended up in one of his journals. It seems that American helicopters had destroyed the Phuoc Tuy Textile Company plant during the Communist Tet Offensive earlier that year. The Viet Cong had taken over the buildings on the plant grounds and used one as a command post and others as fighting positions.

Mang Binh Hao came up with a plan to cheat the American government out of a lot of money because he owned the company that the Americans had destroyed. He went to the South Vietnamese Minister of Finance and filed a claim for damages that amounted to 200 percent of the original cost of his textile plant. Because he was the brother-in-law of the wife of the South Vietnamese president, he was able to get a note from President Quoch to accompany the claim, in order to put pressure on the U.S. government to pay up. After they did, Mang Binh Hao rebuilt the textile plant with half of the money and put the other half in the bank. The men Henri sat close to in the restaurant that evening had a big laugh over that. They called the big-nosed Americans stupid, along with a few other unkind things.

That had been one of the first of several stories Henri wrote down in his journals about Hao. He'd also heard that the President's wife and Hao fronted the President's multi-million dollar corruption scemes. They were the ones who put large amounts of money into different Quoch bank accounts in Singapore and Switzerland. They were also alleged to have made silent-partner investments in Taiwan, Guam and Hawaii. If only I had hard evidence, Henri wished to himself.

One thing was for sure, Hao was smart enough to avoid being caught doing anything illegal. He was using middle-men to keep his name clear, the same way President Quoch was. He'd bought some land in Taiwan and laundered money by being a silent-partner in some of Guam's largest building developments and land holdings. He'd even bought several hundred acres of land in Hawaii by using ill-gotten gains and middle-men.

Henri had seen tons of brass shell casings and other metal scrap from military sources that were brought to the Newport dock his company used. He suspected, but didn't know for sure, that Mang Binh Hao was personally taking payment for the scrap metal out at sea where he met with some of the buyers. All he knew for sure was, whenever Hao would say, "We go over business records," Hao would give him the figures for the records and insist that they were the correct ones to be used.

He didn't dare challenge him on those, even though his figures never matched those that Hao gave him. He knew better than to do that because of what Hao was capable of.

He thought back to 1970 when Vietnamese tax investigators began looking into the tax returns of Hao and business associates of his that were suspected of illegal business practices. Shortly afterwards, the main tax office in downtown Saigon was fire-bombed and burned to the ground. The police report listed Viet Cong sabotage as the reason for the attack.

What had really happened that day was known to only a handful of people, including Henri. That was because Hao had actually bragged about having arranged it, right here in his office, only a few days after the incident.

There were gangs of Vietnamese called tongs or triads in Saigon. They were groups of hard-core thugs, sort of like the old Chinese gangs that controlled vice in Chinese cities before Mao and his Communist Party followers took over. Some of those gangs could be hired to do just about anything for a price. Hao bragged to him that his hired help had taken care of the tax problem. He had an idea as to why Hao told him that. It was a message meant just for him...nobody messes with Mang Binh Hao. Message received.

CHAPTER 3

　　First Lieutenant Tom Ross and the 160 passengers from the Continental Airlines flight that had just landed, were herded into the big passenger terminal. The Air Force sergeant who had greeted them on the plane, led them to the area they were to sit in. There was a big section full of empty multi-colored plastic and chrome seats, waiting for the next group of weary travelers. It had been a long and tiring flight from Travis Air Force Base, California to Tan Son Nhut Air Base, Republic of South Vietnam. The base and international airport was on the northwest side of Saigon.
　　As Lieutenant Ross looked around the terminal at his new surroundings, he gratefully inhaled the cooler, almost odor-free air. The walk from the aircraft parking ramp to the terminal had filled his lungs with hot humid air and jet fuel exhaust odors.
　　His slightly wrinkled Khaki 1505s now had visible sweat marks in the center of his back and under his arms. While he tried to get comfortable in the hard plastic seat, he turned his head from side to side and noticed

that most of his fellow passengers had also experienced the same effects of the high temperatures and humidity common in this part of Southeast Asia.

"Welcome to Vietnam. Get used to it," he muttered under his breath to himself.

An Army corporal walked up to the sergeant who was in charge of this group of passengers. They both wore jungle fatigues. He'd come from another part of the terminal and wasn't a part of this group. He spoke in very low tones so only the sergeant could hear.

"Is there a First Lieutenant Ross here?" the sergeant asked, loud enough for the entire group to hear.

"Yeah, over here!" Ross raised his hand so they could see him. He was sitting on the back row of chairs in the large seating area.

"Sir, Corporal Henderson here was sent to meet you and take you to your billet. Please go with him now, sir." The rest of what he said was directed at the rest of the group.

"The rest of you will be escorted over to the baggage carousel momentarily. Then we'll all meet right back here after you get your luggage. Thank you."

First Lieutenant Tom Ross, United States Air Force, stood up with briefcase in hand and walked over to where the much taller, Corporal Jim Henderson, United States Army, was waiting for him. This is very unusual, Ross thought, to be met at the airport by someone in the Army instead of the Air Force. I sure wasn't expecting that.

Corporal Henderson appeared to be about six foot six at least, he estimated. Ross was five-nine and thought "Stringbean" would be a suitable nickname for the tall and skinny man dressed in green. He smiled at the thought.

Henderson returned the smile, thinking that

he was meeting a friendly officer for a change. A lot of the officers he'd been sent to pick up at the terminal were all business and wouldn't greet him with a smile or any kind of friendly gesture.

"Sir, I'm Corporal Henderson and I've been sent here ta give ya a ride to your quarters. If ya got any baggage, just give me the baggage tag stubs and I'll go get 'em for ya." His accent was most definetly Southern.

Lieutenant Ross was holding his briefcase in his left hand and offered his right hand for a friendly handshake. One thing he'd learned from his previous experiences with enlisted men was that officers who treated their men with respect and genuinely cared about them, could get the same in return and then some. Officers could be both friendly and professional. Problem was, there weren't enough officers like that, at least not in his experiences.

He gave Corporal Henderson the two baggage tag stubs he'd had in his briefcase and gave him a description of his suitcases. While waiting for his return, Ross stood there looking around at the different sights within the terminal.

He saw civilians in one area that were sitting in seats just like the one he'd been sitting in. He guessed they were waiting to board the huge Air France 747 that was parked near his smaller Continental B-707.

He observed several Vietnamese women with short-handled, long-bristled straw brooms and dust pans. They were walking around keeping the floor litter-free. They wore the traditional black silk pants, white blouses and conical straw hats that were held on their upper backs by strips of cloth tied loosely around their necks. Other Vietnamese working in the terminal wore Western-style clothing like their American co-workers.

He also noticed many men in uniform milling about, representing all branches of the U.S. military forces. There were a couple of Austrailian soldiers too, easily distinguished by their bush hats with one side pinned up flat.

There were some South Vietnamese soldiers and airmen in the terminal as well. He stared at a couple of them when he noticed they were holding hands. He'd never seen men holding hands before and it struck him as being very strange. He didn't know if they were a couple of homosexuals or if that was something culturally acceptable, unique to Vietnam. It just didn't look right to him.

Corporal Henderson was back with his two gray, medium-size suitcases sooner than he expected.

"Here they are, sir. Just follow me and I'll lead the way out ta the parkin' lot."

"OK, thanks."

Ross felt like a halfback following behind a pulling guard during a football game as the tall corporal cleared a path through the terminal on the way to the parking lot-side of the building.

It seemed like only yesterday that he'd been carrying a football in his left hand instead of a briefcase, running from the T-formation his coach was so fond of. He'd played football in high school and college in Oklahoma before entering the Air Force. My, how time flies when you're having fun, he thought, as the past faded away and the oppressive heat and humidity of the parking lot quickly brought him back to the present.

Henderson put his suitcases in the back floorboard of a jeep. It was a standard olive drab-colored U.S. Army jeep with a white star stenciled on the hood and registration numbers on the sides. The steering wheel was chained with a heavy-duty padlock holding it in place. Vehicle thefts had been a big problem throughout the country.

Ross noticed that Corporal Henderson was wearing a sidearm. The pistol was in a holster on a web belt and hung on his right hip. Right after Henderson removed the chain from the steering wheel, he removed the web belt with the holstered gun. Then he held it out to Ross.

"Sir, would ya take this? You're ridin' shotgun this trip." Henderson then started the jeep and backed out of the parking space. They were on their way.

"There's been some attacks on military vehicles in Saigon by VC on motorcycles. We call 'em 'Cowboys.' They ride in pairs. One does the drivin' and the guy in back does the shootin' or tosses a grenade."

He took a quick look to his right to see if the LT was listening. By the look on his face, he knew he had his undivided attention.

"We have to carry a weapon at all times when we leave the motor pool and since my hands are busy steerin' and changin' gears, it's better if the passenger has the pistol and rides shotgun, just like in the old Wild West movies."

"OK. And that means I'd better be looking around and paying attention to the motorcycles that get close to us, huh?"

"Yes, sir. And be ready ta unsnap the holster cover, take the gun out, chamber a round, take the safety off as quick as ya can and don't miss when ya shoot."

He was grinning when he said all that. Hell, that would be a challenge even for Wyatt Earp, he thought.

"This is the Army standard-issue model 1911A .45 caliber semi-automatic, right?"

"Yes, sir. Ever fire one before?"

"Only once. A relative of mine had one and I got to shoot a whole clip one day. It had quite a kick. I was trained on the M-16 and the .38 caliber revolver at Air Force firing ranges. I'm sure I still remember how to shoot this little cannon. I didn't shoot well enough to get the expert marksman ribbon but I did hit the targets enough to qualify."

"That's good, sir. Let's hope ya don't have ta use it today but if ya do, be fast on the draw."

"I'll be ready. I want to live to be a very old man."

"Me too, sir," he replied, with all seriousness.

Ross thought about the situation he was now in for a moment. I never would have imagined that, on my very first day in Vietnam, I'd be holding a gun and watching out for an attack by the Viet Cong on motorcycles. He reflected on that thought for a moment.

"Where exactly are we going, Corporal Henderson?"

As they neared one of the gates that led out of the base into Saigon, Henderson answered, "The BOQ over on Cong Ly Boulevard, sir. There's a lotta buildings scattered all over Saigon that Uncle Sam rents from the Vietnamese ta use as billets. Some are only for enlisted men, others are just for officers."

They stopped briefly at the gate when the South Vietnamese MP put his hand up. When he saw Lieutenant Ross, he quickly came to attention and rendered a snappy salute. As soon as Ross returned the salute, the guard waved them through.

"Where are you from back in the States? I thought I detected a Southern accent."

That was putting it mildly. I bet he could do a great imitation of Gomer Pyle, that character on the Andy Griffith TV show, Ross amusedly thought.

"Blakely, Georgia. Ever hear of it, sir?"

"No, can't say that I have. What part of Georgia is it in? Anywhere near Atlanta?" That was the only city in Georgia he could think of at the moment.

"No, sir. Far from it." *He obviously don't know nuthin' 'bout Georgia.* "It's way down in the southwest part, between Dothan, Alabama and Albany, Georgia. It's about a hour drive south a Fort Bennin', the big Army base near Columbus."

"Yeah, I've heard of Fort Benning." *Who hasn't?*

"How 'bout yourself, sir? Where ya'll from?" Henderson asked, as he down-shifted into a lower gear and hit the brakes.

He was trying hard not to run into a Vespa-like motorscooter with two people on it that had suddenly slowed down in front of them. The woman on the back had a woven straw basket of vegetables in both arms. No Viet Cong to worry about there. The traffic was very congested now with motorbikes, scooters and motorcycles weaving in and out of each lane that had taxis, delivery trucks, even big Army deuce-and-a-halfs, all trying to get somewhere at the same time. Typical, every-day Saigon traffic.

"I was born and raised in Del City, Oklahoma. It's just a few miles southeast of Oklahoma City. It seems so far away, like I'm on a different planet now, if you know what I mean."

"Oh, yes sir. I know exactly what ya mean. It'll take a while, but ya get used ta it. After a while, ya won't even notice how different it smells here."

As he said that, Henderson turned towards Ross and wrinkled up his nose and made a face, as if he'd just smelled a rotten fart.

That got a good laugh from Ross. He replied, "Yeah, I did notice that this place smells a lot worse than any place I've ever been." With the Oklahoma City stockyards being the only exception, he told himself, as an after-thought.

He was about to ask how much further they had to go to reach the BOQ on Cong Ly Boulevard when they pulled over to the curb. They'd been traveling for at least twenty minutes and he was looking forward to taking a shower, changing into some clean clothes and most of all, a chance to rest his travel-weary body in a comfortable bed.

They were now parked in front of a tall brick structure that reminded him of an apartment building he'd once seen in Oklahoma City that had an air conditioner sticking out of each window. The only noticeable difference was, this building had sandbagged gun positions on either side of the main entrance. There were armed South Vietnamese soldiers manning both positions.

"Well, here we are, sir, 192 Cong Ly Boulevard, your new home-away-from home. I'll get your bags and when we get inside, ya just check in at the front desk just like ya would at a hotel back in the world. They'll ask ya for a copy of orders, assign ya a room and tell ya what time ta be back down in the lobby."

As they walked down the sidewalk towards the main entrance, Henderson again led the way.

"Usually somebody from your new unit will be here the next day or so and take ya ta get signed in, meet your new commander and first shirt and stuff like that."

After setting the lieutenant's suitcases down near the check-in counter, Corporal

Henderson said, "I'll take that gun back now, sir. It's time for me ta get back over ta the motor pool. Welcome ta Vietnam, Lieutenant."

"Thanks," replied Ross. "Nice meeting you and thanks for the ride, Corporal Henderson. Drive safe!" he said with a smile.

"Will do, sir!" They shook hands again and Henderson was out the door in a few long strides. He was thinking about a lunch break now, a big juicy cheeseburger and fries.

As Corporal Henderson removed the chain from the steering wheel of the jeep, he thought about the Air Force officer he'd just given a ride to. That was a pretty decent guy. Too bad the Army officers I work for aren't more like that. How'd the Army end up with so many dipsticks anyway?

He hadn't told the Lieutenant one important event that he'd been told about regarding this particular BOQ. He didn't want to worry the guy too much since he just got here. Back in 1968, the VC attacked this Bachelor Officer Quarters. Three American MPs, three Vietnamese police and ten Viet Cong died in the attack. One hundred and thirteen Americans were wounded. Yeah, he thought, it's better that story was left untold. Besides, it probably wouldn't happen again.

Lieutenant Ross had gotten the shower, change of clothes and rest he badly needed. Now, on the morning of his first full day in-country, he went down to the lobby of his billet on Cong Ly Boulevard to see if he'd gotten any messages from his new unit. He hoped that whoever might come here to pick him up would take him somewhere to get some breakfast on the way to reporting in. He had not eaten a thing since the last meal served on the plane that brought him here and he was starving. The image of that hot roast beef sandwich with melted cheese they'd served him yesterday was appearing in full living color in his mind, along with its smell and taste and it was driving him crazy.

"Good morning. Any messages for me?" he asked the clerk behind the check-in counter.

"Good morning, sir." The clerk looked at his uniform name tag, asked for his room number, then turned around to check the message board. Sure enough, there was a message thumbtacked to the cork board for 1Lt. Tom Ross, USAF.

"Here you are, sir. Somebody called a while ago. I took the message myself."

"Thanks."

He read the brief message that was printed neatly on a small slip of paper: 1Lt. Ross, rest up today, will pick you up at 0700 in the lobby tomorrow. From Capt. Daniels.

He stuck the piece of paper in his pants pocket, relieved that he could now eat before doing anything else.

The billet had its own dining hall on the ground floor and, having been told of its location yesterday when he checked in, went straight there.

An hour later he was back in his second-floor room. Having devoured a large breakfast at a leisurely pace, he was ready to change into a T-shirt, gym shorts and just lounge around in his room for the rest of the day. Despite the coffee he drank with his meal, jet lag was already starting to affect him. He could tell that his normal energy level just wasn't up to par yet as he changed clothes.

He turned on the old black and white TV

set in his room and caught the tail-end of the morning news on the pre-set Armed Forces TV network channel. When an old rerun of Gunsmoke came on next, he turned it off and plopped down on his bed. The reading material his neighbor in Oklahoma had given him last week was still on the small nightstand within reach.

Randy Smith had returned from Vietnam a changed man in some ways. He and his neighbors used to talk almost every day. Now he hardly talked to anyone at all.

He did two tours of duty with the 1st Infantry Division, the famed Big Red One. After returning home from his second tour, he decided to go back to being a civilian again. He could not stand the thought of possibly having to do another tour in what he called "the armpit of the world." Hell no!

He could be seen every evening sitting on his back porch, sipping a cold beer and just staring off at something in the far distance. His old frame house, inheirited from his deceased parents, was badly in need of a fresh coat of white paint. It was only a few feet away from the Ross family home in a quiet neighborhood where all the houses were fairly close together.

One evening he saw Ross taking out the garbage for his parents and invited him over. He was in one of his better moods and felt like talking for a change. He'd heard that Ross had recently gotten orders for 'Nam and was home on leave. Ross knew Randy had been there already and looked forward to the opportunity to ask him a few questions about it.

It seemed like only yesterday when those conversations took place. Looking over at the nightstand, Ross remembered the day he became the new owner of the government-

published reading material. Randy had told
him that the stuff was just some souvineers
and he didn't want them anymore. After hearing that Ross was headed for Vietnam, he
urged him to read them all.

One of the publications was called TOUR
365, given to Army troops, "grunts like me,"
Randy had said, who finished their one-year
tours, hence the title. It had lots of
color photos, some of unit patches, U.S.
medals and Vietnamese awards that were given
to American GIs.

He remembered Randy telling him how a
fellow passenger on his plane ride home and
in the Air Force like Ross, had given him
the publication called MISSION VIETNAM. It
was, in some ways, similar to TOUR 365, with
lots of photos, but was made for members of
the Air Force. It had lots of pictures of
different Air Force aircraft and Air Force
personnel performing various jobs throughout
Vietnam.

The publication that interested Ross the
most though, was a small, pocket-size booklet
called POCKET GUIDE TO VIETNAM. It had a lot
of information about the history of Vietnam,
the different ethnic backgrounds of its
people and diverse cultures and religions,
with lots of black and white photos. There
were tips on "Do's and Don'ts" along with
some Vietnamese words and phrases, with English translations.

So far, Ross had only looked at some of
the pictures. With a whole day off now, he
could relax and read through the publications
from cover to cover. He hoped that he might
find something that would help him, one way
or another, during his own tour of duty here.

Some of the stories that Randy had shared
with him over the course of a few beers might
even help him somehow too. In one of the

stories, Randy had said that O-1 "Birddog" spotter planes had dropped thousands of leaflets over some villages thought to harbor some Viet Cong. The leaflets were printed in Vietnamese and had some drawings on them. They instructed the reader to bring it to any South Vietnamese or American military unit and they'd be well-treated. It was part of the Cheu Hoi or Open Arms Program.

Some former Viet Cong had surrendered that way and then worked for American units as "Kit Carson" scouts. Now, instead of trying to kill GIs, they were showing them where to find hidden weapons caches, VC tax collectors and stuff like that.

Randy advised him that, if he ever got the chance to work with one of those former VC, he should take full advantage of their knowledge and expertise.

Ross finished unpacking his stuff before he went to sleep that night. He placed his tan Western-style boots, the kind some people call "cowboy boots," on the floor under his bed right next to his military shoes and boots. They were just plain work boots to him, not the fancy hand-tooled leather dressy kind some guys wore to church.

His favorite belt was coiled up inside one of the boots. It was a wide leather one that matched his tan boots. It had a large silver buckle with his initials engraved in it, a birthday gift from his parents.

He didn't like to wear hats of any kind when not in uniform, not even ball caps. He brought a few pairs of blue jeans and a few pull-over polo shirts with collars and a couple of buttons with him, no suits or dress pants. He liked to travel and pack light. He was from Oklahoma by God and if somebody didn't like the way he dressed, well, that was just too damn bad.

He made a mental note to find a barber shop soon too. He needed a trim to keep his curly brown hair within regulations. He always wore it as long as he was allowed, right up to the limits. That's just the way he was, a maverick in some ways, a straight shooter in others.

It took him awhile to fall asleep in his new surroundings, anxiously wondering what adventures, if any, his new assignment might bring. He wouldn't have to wait long to find out.

CHAPTER 4

It was another bright sunny day, with clear blue skies and not a cloud anywhere in sight. People were going about their business as usual in Saigon as if the war didn't even exist. Those who knew better, thought of it as the calm before the storm.

As Henri sat at his desk and busied himself with some of the paperwork his job required, he thought back to Hao's attempts at small talk during his last visit. It struck him as being a little odd that he had asked him about his daughter, Genevieve. He'd told him her name years ago, back when he explained how his Vietnamese wife, Nguyen Thi Kieu, had been accidently killed during the Buddhist demonstrations in 1963. He never mentioned Genevieve's name to Hao since then.

Now that he thought about it, he felt that the only reason Hao would have mentioned her by name and asked how she was doing, was to make a point of some kind. If only I could read between the lines, he thought. Hao wasn't being nice or polite. That was just Hao being Hao, that SOB!

For years now, he and Genevieve had been making an annual trip to visit his wife's grave in Vung Tau. They did that on the anniversary of her death, which was just a couple of days away. Now, as he sat at his desk, he decided to write her a note and tell her when to meet with him so they could plan their upcoming trip together. As he stared at the blank piece of paper, thinking about the wording of the note, his mind began to wander. He quickly lost focus on the task at hand. A headache, worse than the ones before, caused him to squeeze his eyes shut and wince in pain.

In his mind, he saw a young Vietnamese street vendor, selling fruit and vegetables from a hand cart. Even in the shade of her wide conical straw hat, he saw how pretty she was. He was walking down a street in Vung Tau, having just left his office on his lunch break. He really wasn't interested in what she was selling, but stopped by her cart anyway just so he could see her close up. That was how he met his wife, Nguyen Thi Kieu. He'd been working in Vung Tau since 1947 and in 1949, he found the love of his life.

They got married in 1950 and their only child, Genevieve, was born in 1952. She was half-Vietnamese and half-French and to her father, the most beautiful baby girl in the world. Now he had two beauties in his life and he was a very happy man.

The Gulf of Lion Shipping Company was growing and he was offered a raise and a new position in their larger Saigon regional office. His wife didn't like the idea of leaving the town she was born and raised in and where her ancestors were buried. Ancestors played a big role in Vietnamese culture, he had learned.

He tried to convince her that the treaty

signed in 1954 ended both the war and French colonial rule and now it was much safer to travel the road to Saigon. Plus, they could always return to Vung Tau on visits. He really needed the extra money he'd get in the new job to provide a better life for his family. She finally acquiesced.

They moved from the small coastal city the French had called Cap St. Jacques to the much larger city of Saigon in 1955. Things went very well for the three of them until 1963. They lived in a nice house and could even afford a maid, what GIs would call a mama san, even though the term was coined by GIs in Japan and not Vietnam.

One day Nguyen Thi Kieu and her maid got into an open-air cyclo, a three-wheeled motorcycle taxi, to take a trip to the market. It was something they'd done a couple of times each week whenever they needed to restock the pantry or shop for clothes. On their way back from the market, some government soldiers and police were out in the streets, battling some Buddhist demonstrators. As soon as their driver turned off the main boulevard where the confrontation was taking place and started into a narrow side street to avoid the clash, shots rang out. A stray bullet fired by one of the government troops, hit Kieu in the head. She died on the operating table in the French-run Grall Hospital.

A Buddhist monk set himself on fire at the site of the demonstration that day. His fiery death from self-immolation made the top story on the TV evening news and newspaper headlines around the world. Kieu's death, however, went virtually unnoticed.

Henri remembered that tragic day as if it was only yesterday. His head was pounding, his heart was aching and now he was crying over the loss of his beloved wife again. He silently cursed himself for moving his family to Saigon. Kieu would still be alive if they had remained in Vung Tau and he'd be free from the likes of Mang Binh Hao and this lousy business. Plus, he wouldn't have to worry about Genevieve's safety either.

He removed the handkerchief from his back pocket and wiped away the tears from his face. Then he stopped by the front office on his way out of the building.

"Miss Xuan, I'm going to Grall Hospital for a check-up because of my worsening headaches. I'll be back tomorrow morning."

It was already mid-afternoon and none of their ships were in port at the moment. The paperwork on his desk would just have to wait.

"Yes, Mr. Ferrand. I hope you will feel better soon," replied the company's head secretary in French, the language they always used when speaking to eachother. For all his years in Vietnam, he still wasn't as well-versed in her language as she was in his.

Still in pain, Henri managed a smile as he approached the front entrance of the hospital. About to exit through the same door was an old friend of his, Ngai Bien Phong, whom he recognized instantly. They had met in Marseille, France many years ago. Now his friend, who held dual citizenship in both France and South Vietnam, had risen to the position of Minister of National Defense under the current regime. A couple of army officers served as his armed escorts that accompanied him every time he left his office. Today was no exception.

Henri waited just outside the door until they exited so they could greet eachother and not cause a scene by their loud exchange.

"Bonjour, Phong!"

A second later, after his eyes adjusted to the bright sunlight and he recognized the greeter, he cried out in delight, "Bonjour, mon ami!"

Phong embraced his old friend in a hug and they patted eachother on the back before stepping back to look eachother over as old friends often do when they haven't seen eachother in a while. The escort officers had stepped back to give them some space once they were certain the minister was in no danger. They didn't know who the foreigner was, but it was clear that their boss did.

Henri and Phong had both been born in Marseille and therefore spoke French with the same accent. Henri was only a couple of years older than Phong, who still looked trim and fit.

"So, Henri, my friend, what brings you to the hospital today?" asked the diminutive minister.

"I've been having bad headaches for awhile and they seem to be getting worse over time," he explained, still forcing a smile. "It is truely good to see you again, mon ami. And you, what brings you here?"

"Oh, just an annual physical exam, that's all. And your daughter, how is she doing after losing her mother in that tragic way?" He still remembered the terrible news from Henri's letter he'd received years ago.

"Would you believe, she's almost twenty years old now and operates her own tour guide business?" he stated proudly. "She's doing well but misses her mother terribly, as I do," he said, with a bit of sadness in his tone and a slight change of expression.

"Well Henri, you know what they say. Time heals all wounds. And best of luck with your headache problem."

"Thank you. And how about you? Are the rumors true, about you running for president I mean?"

He hoped his friend would run against the corrupt President Trung Ho Quoch in the next election. It seemed there wasn't anything his friend couldn't do once he put his mind to it. Rumors abounded in Saigon about who might run in the next election.

"Being the Minister of National Defense is enough of a headache for me, no pun intended," Phong replied. "We don't get enough say at the Paris Peace Talks, the American, Australian, Philippine and South Korean allies are all going home and there are too many internal problems within our military leadership and politicians. No, when my term is up, I'm seriously thinking of writing a book about my life and spend the rest of it in retirement. It was so good to see you again, Henri. I've got to get back to work now, so if you'll excuse me, I really must be going now," Phong politely stated. "Stay in touch, Henri."

"I will."

They shook hands while saying their goodbyes and then went their separate ways.

While he sat in the waiting room, patiently listening for his name to be called, Henri thought about what Phong had said regarding writing a book about his life. He certainly has had an interesting life, worthy of a good book, he reasoned.

Ngai Bien Phong was born in Marseilles, France. His father was a doctor and his mother was a teacher. He graduated from a French university and served in the French Army in World War II. First he fought against the Germans in France, then in 1944 he traveled to French Indochina to fight the Japanese. After the war, he returned to France to attend the French Army Command and Staff College. He was appointed Chief of Military Security and then later he became the Chief of Staff of the South Vietnamese Army. In the late 1960s, he was appointed Minister of National Defense. For a man who was only five feet one inch in height, he stood tall among all men in his accomplishments.

Yes, he thought, this friend whom he'd first met in Marseille so many years ago, had certainly lived a life worth writing about. Thankfully, he wouldn't be writing about him in any of his journals as he did with so many others in positions of authority. Too bad this country doesn't have more men like him, he sadly reflected.

CHAPTER 5

Navy Lieutenants Bob Kosinski and Daniel Ventnor had just returned from their first assignment as members of the 1st Special Investigations Unit (SIU). Their flight back to Tan Son Nhut aboard an Air Force C-130 had been as uneventful as the investigation itself.

"Good to see you guys again. So, how'd it go, Bob?" asked their CO, Captain Greg Daniels.

He hoped they got some information they could work with. He was in his civvies today, as were the rest of the investigative members of the unit. Only the support personnel were required to work in uniforms. Unless directed by someone higher up, that was the way it was going to be in the 1st SIU. Since they were in his office with the door closed for the debrief and away from the enlisted men, they were free to talk on a first name basis.

"I think we were able to eliminate Phu Bai from the list of places where the drugs may have been put in that Marine Lance Corporal's casket. Daniel and I think someone in the

Tan Son Nhut mortuary was most likely the culprit," Bob stated matter of factly.

"Daniel, how did you guys arrive at that conclusion?" Greg inquired, curious about the other lieutenant's opinion.

"Well, Greg," the lanky Virginian said with a noticeable Southern accent, "we snooped around some, asked a lot of folks up there some questions and figured that, if the drugs had been put in the casket there, somebody at either Da Nang or Tan Son Nhut would have discovered them. Since the plane that carried the Marine's casket had flown from Tan Son Nhut to Clark, odds are greater that the drugs were put in the casket at the Tan Son Nhut mortuary. And by the way, the mortuaries at Da Nang and Tan Son Nhut are both run by the Army, so our suspect is most likely in the Army."

Daniel was satisfied with himself for having answered the question so thoroughly and glad that his fellow investigator was shaking his head in agreement.

"I'm inclined to agree with you. However, I'm still curious about what the mortuary in Phu Bai was like. Tell me something about that, Bob."

Greg had noticed that Bob looked like he was chomping at the bit to add something to what Daniel had just said, so he directed his inquiry to him.

Bob was only an inch or two shorter than Daniel but was much stockier. He'd played football at Boston College on a scholarship before getting his commission through their NROTC program. He and Daniel were both single, in their mid-twenties and worked well together. Not bad for a Yankee and a Rebel, Bob thought. He only wished that Daniel would stop showing off his Naval Academy class ring as if it was an Olympic gold medal.

Except for that minor irretation, he was an OK guy in his book.

He spoke with only a slight Boston accent, pronouncing the word "far" as "fah", as if it had no letter r in it.

"The Graves Registration Unit of the Third Medical Battalion, Third Marine Division, was in a building far from the airfield, and I mean **real** far. It looked just like all the rest of the buildings nearby, built out of wood with a corrugated tin roof."

He paused just long enough to take another sip of coffee from the mug he'd been holding since he first sat down. He noticed that Greg had been nodding his head, indicating that he was paying attention when he was talking. Then he continued with his description.

"There was a large, mobile refrigeration unit attached to the rear of the building. They had three layers of sandbags stacked up for protection around each side of the building too. The Graves Registration Unit was staffed completely by Marines."

He paused again and took another sip of his now barely-warm coffee.

"When the dead came into Phu Bai from the field, they were brought directly to Graves Registration. They were washed down, identified, and put in the refrigeration unit until they were flown to either Tan Son Nhut or Da Nang. Then they were embalmed and flown back to the US of A."

Right after that last sentence, Bob drained the last of his coffee and paused again, giving his CO a chance to interject another question.

"So, did you guys get to see any casualties arrive from the field while you were there?"

Daniel jumped in with the answer.

"No, thank God, we didn't. I don't think I

would have had the stomach for that."

"Me either," chimed in Bob. "It was bad enough just to be in that building at all. The place gave me the creeps, even though it was kept real clean and everything. We only stayed in there long enough to look around some, ask a few questions, then we got the hell out of there."

All three officers laughed a little after that last comment.

"Well, rest easy, gentlemen. I'm not sending you over to the mortuary at Tan Son Nhut. That assignment will go to our former Army CID guys."

Captain Daniels saw a look of relief on the faces of the two Navy investigators as soon as he told them that.

"You get to check on some Navy personnel next, right here in Saigon," he announced with a smile.

He knew they'd prefer this new assignment over the alternatives.

"Let me give you a little background information first. You guys have heard that saying, 'Loose lips sink ships,' right?"

They both nodded their heads in the affirmative.

"Well, a civilian, who used to be a Navy SEAL, was overheard in a bar in Norfolk, Virginia, telling his drinking buddies some bad-ass war stories about himself and his team in Vietnam. What he didn't realize was, in the booth right behind him were a couple of off-duty Naval Intel guys. When he began bragging about his involvement in smuggling heroin out of Vietnam, it got the attention of his NCIS neighbors big time. That's how we got our tip for your next assignment."

Greg then paused for a long sip of coffee from his mug that was now almost empty. He looked at both Navy men and saw their brown eyes light up in anticipation.

"You guys are going to love this. It seems that Navy SEAL teams about to leave Vietnam, have a favorite bar they all go to for one last going-away party. The place is called Linda's Surprise Bar, right on the outskirts of Saigon. We're not sure yet, but it's possible that that's where they're getting their drugs from too."

"So we get to hang out in a bar every night as part of our assignment?" asked an incredulous Bob Kosinski, thinking it was too good to be true.

Before Greg had a chance to answer him, Daniel Ventnor asked, "What kind of place is it anyway?" He couldn't hide the excitement in his voice at all.

"I've been told that Linda's Surprise Bar puts on live sex shows for GIs. Because the owner pays off the authorities to look the other way, they haven't been shut down. There are laws against this type of illicit activity but they make so much money, they can afford to make big pay-offs. So, you won't have to worry about police raids, but you may have to watch out for drunken Navy SEALS, which could be even worse," Greg advised.

"Starting tonight, you'll both be hanging out in Linda's Surprise Bar as part of your assignment. Find out if anyone on the SEAL teams is involved in drug smuggling. Who knows, maybe you'll even be able to identify the suppliers as well, which would be a bonus. How's that for an exciting investigative assignment?" Greg asked, noticing Bob and Daniel's huge smiles.

"Can't wait to get started, Greg," replied the eager Virginian, Daniel.

"That goes for me too," added his equally eager partner, Bob.

"OK guys, we need some results ASAP. The commander of MACV asks me almost every day if we've accomplished something that's making a difference in the drug smuggling problem and I can't keep telling him, 'Not yet, sir, but we're working on it.' That answer is getting old real quick and I don't like to sound like a broken record. Go get some rest guys, 'cause with your new work schedule, you're going to need it!"

With that said, Captain Daniels stood up and shook their hands and led them out of his office. He was headed for the coffee pot in the main office for a refill before the next team of investigators showed up. As for the two Navy lieutenants, they were headed for trouble. They just didn't know it yet.

Man, why couldn't I get an assignment like that when I was young and single, Daniels mused. Imagine that, getting to drink cold beer and watch a hot sex show while on the job. Some guys just have all the luck! Now I'm too old for that shit and all I get is a bunch of reports to write and a ton of paperwork to do every day. No wonder I drink so much coffee, he thought, as he stirred in some sugar and powdered creamer into his third cup of the day.

CHAPTER 6

    Henri Ferrand was temporarily in a good mood. Earlier in the evening, he and his daughter, Genevieve, had gotten together for a meal to discuss their upcoming annual trip to Vung Tau. Each year they visited his wife's grave in the cemetery of her ancestors, on the anniversary of her death. Henri was emotionally torn between the solemn affair of visiting the gravesite and the joy of spending time with his grown daughter during the trip. Ever since she'd started her own tour guide business, he didn't get to see her as often as he'd like. Genevieve was possessed by an entrepreneurial spirit, just like her mother had been.
    These annual pilgrimages always caused Henri to become an emotional mess. First he broke down and cried at his wife's grave because he missed her so much. Right after he placed the colorful flowers on her grave and Genevieve lit the fragrant incense sticks, that's when the tears would begin to flow.
    The feelings he had for his wife, Nguyen Thi Kieu, went far beyond the purely physical intimacy that a man enjoyed with a loving

wife. It was only natural for him to think of those special times whenever he became lonely and he missed those intimate moments with her a lot. They had been very compatible in the bedroom for two people who were from very different cultural and religious backgrounds. Vive la difference! It was the deep love and respect they'd developed for eachother that transcended everything that was different about the two of them and made them as one.

The birth of their daughter had brought them much joy. Genevieve had been named after Henri's grandmother, becoming the third Genevieve Ferrand in his family tree. Now, she was a young woman and at the end of each annual trip when they said their goodbyes, he broke down and cried again. Unconditional love for a wife and a daughter can do that to a man. At least it did to Henri Ferrand.

As he sipped his after-dinner demitasse and savored the heavenly chocolate eclair that he so craved, Henri reminisced about the times he and his daughter had spent together. Except for a younger brother in France, she was the only family he had. And now, he feared for her life, more now than ever before.

Years ago, Mang Binh Hao had told him that if he went along with the business deals his shipping company was involved in, his family would be protected and kept safe from any harm. However, their lives **wouldn't** be protected and kept safe if he didn't go along with things. Therefore, he feared for all their lives. Now things had changed and in very unsettling ways.

His doctor had recently given him some ominously bad news. After doing extensive testing to determine what was causing the headaches that got progressively worse over time, they had discovered a cancerous brain tumor that was considered inoperable. It was too early to tell just how much time he had left to live, his doctor had told him. He had been so stunned by the news that he found to be down right terrifying, that he couldn't recall most of what else the doctor had said to him that day. He just remembered hearing the word "sorry" being used over and over again. He had not told Genevieve anything about the exceptionally disturbing news yet.

If that wasn't bad enough, an acquaintance of his gave him some more bad news. As he sat in Givral, his favorite restaurant in downtown Saigon, enjoying a few moments alone to ponder his fate, Bui Van Nha sat down across from him at his small table near a front window.

Bui Van Nha was a former captain in the South Vietnamese Army. He had lost his right hand in battle and was given a medical discharge. Because he had shown great courage in leading his troops on the battlefield and was a favorite of his commanding officer, he was able to receive several favorable recommendations to help him get a job working for South Vietnam's Central Intelligence Agency. It didn't matter to them that he had only one hand.

Nha's office was just off Hai Ba Trung Street, on the banks of the Saigon River, next to the Navy Headquarters building near Newport Bridge. It was within easy walking distance of Henri's office. That made it easy for him to monitor the comings and goings of the owner of the Phuoc Tuy Textile Company and the Gulf of Lion Shipping Company, Mang Binh Hao.

"Hello, Henri."

"Hello, Nha. Would you care for some coffee or perhaps an eclair?"

"No, thank you, I've already eaten. I

happened to see you sitting alone as I was passing by and decided to talk to you about something very important."

Sure, Nha. You just happened to be in the neighborhood. What a coincidence! I wonder how long he's been following me, Henri thought.

Nha was dressed in such a way that he could easily blend in with the general population of males in the city. He wore a short sleeve white cotton dress shirt, dark gray dress pants and sandals, the same thing that thousands of Vietnamese men wore in Saigon every day. His black hair was a little longer now than when he was in the Army. He was of average height and weight for a Vietnamese male and most Westerners would not have been able to pick him out of a police line-up due to their "they all look the same to me" vision of Asians. Only the missing right hand made him uniquely different and he kept that fact well hidden most of the time. In his new line of work, blending in with the rest of society was in his best interest.

The thirty-three year old Nha had been investigating corruption within the South Vietnamese military establishment and in a roundabout way, had discovered that Henri's boss, Mang Binh Hao, was one of the most corrupt individuals with government connections. He was hoping that Henri would be able to provide him with some evidence that he could use against Hao. He thought that by telling Henri a few things that would be of interest to him, he might be able to get his cooperation, a sort of trade-off, a "you scratch my back, I'll scratch yours" type of arrangement.

Henri sensed that Nha was up to his old tricks again. He had a habit of starting to say something, like when he just said, "... talk to you about something very important," and then he'd just sit there and not say anything at all, just looking at you as if to say, "Now it's your turn to say something."

Henri fell for it every time, even though he knew it was coming. It was just part of the game that Nha played, knowing the other person's curiosity would get the best of them every time. He gave Nha a friendly smile and once again decided to play along.

"What is it you want to tell me, Nha?"

"I know that you are afraid to tell me what you know about Mang Binh Hao. If he ever found out that you told me about his illegal business arrangements, he'd probably have you killed, or maybe your daughter, or both of you. We both know he's a ruthless man, yes?"

"D'accord."

"What I want to tell you today is not good. Not for you or for me either."

He had a very serious look on his face and it made Henri very uncomfortable. Nha paused once again, his way of building up suspense. It was starting to irretate Henri at this point.

"Go on, continue, s'il vous plait."

"I have spoken with some people, very knowledgeable people, who are members of the Provisional Revolutionary Government, run by the Viet Cong. They do not know that I work for the CIA. They think that I'm just a disgruntled, out of work, former Army officer, a decorated war veteran who lost a hand in combat and is very dissatisfied with the current government."

Nha had to stop talking when a waiter approached their table. He knew the dangers of speaking about certain topics in public. There were spies and double-agents all over Saigon. He and Henri both ordered a cup of tea so they could stay at their table awhile longer.

"I've been told," Nha continued, after taking a sip of tea, "the government of South Vietnam will collapse soon after all the Americans have left. After the Communists take over, they will round up all the people who did business with the corrupt military and civilian leaders of the government. Anyone with ties to the South Vietnamese government will be in great danger."

There was an ominous tone in Nha's voice and his face was strained with emotion and fear when he said that. His life would be in jeopardy too, for obvious reasons.

Henri was looking directly at Nha's face and he could tell that this was not something that was being said to coerce him into saying something about Hao. At least that's what he thought. It seemed to him that Nha was being very pragmatic about the whole situation. Now Henri knew, he was caught between a rock and a hard spot. If he turned over his journals and told Nha everything he knew about Hao and his cronies, Hao might find out and have his daughter, or the both of them, killed. On the other hand, when the Communists took over, the same fate awaited them. Either way, he was going to die. The only question was, would his cancerous brain tumor kill him first and leave Genevieve to face her fate alone? He was facing a very precarious dilemma.

Leaving the country would not be possible. He knew that Hao and others that worked for him, kept an eye on him at all times. He was not even sure if Nha was on Hao's payroll or not. For all he knew, Hao could be paying Nha to trick him into telling him things and that is why he said that he was investigating Hao and his associates. It could be a well-devised trap.

Nha reached down with his left hand and rubbed the end of his right arm where his other hand used to be. It sometimes felt as if his right hand or individual fingers were itching, moving slightly, as if the hand was still there.

Seeing that Henri wasn't responding to what he'd just told him, he looked him right in the eyes, something he rarely ever did when talking to someone. Henri seemed to be daydreaming, staring off into the distance as if he wasn't even there.

"Henri, are you OK? Did you hear what I just said?"

"Yes, oh yes, I heard you. Sorry, it's just so much to think about, that's all."

"Well, you think about it some more and if you wish to tell me anything about Hao, you know where to find me. My office isn't far from yours, you know."

"I just have one question before you go. Do you **really** believe the Communists will win this war shortly after the Americans leave?" Henri asked, with a follow-up question in mind.

"Yes, Henri, unfortunately, I truely believe that," replied Nha, with all the sincerity he could muster.

"Can you tell me why? Things seem to be going well now."

"I will tell you why, but you must promise me to never repeat what I'm about to tell you," Nha said, barely above a whisper.

"OK, I promise," answered Henri, also barely above a whisper.

"Move your chair in a little closer and lean in because I must whisper to make sure nobody else will hear what I'm saying."

Henri complied, wondering what the big secret was that he was about to be told and if it would be true.

Nha began explaining things in earnest. "First of all, corruption has become a way of life throughout the highest ranks of the military. Many colonels and generals are political appointees, having been placed in their jobs by very corrupt politicians. There are a few exceptions to this, but by and large, the majority of our top military leaders are inept cowards, even traitors."

He stopped whispering for a moment as a waiter came to their table and refilled their cups with more hot tea. Most of Givral's waiters were middle-aged men with many years of experience at their jobs and the service here was first-class in every way. They added to the French-influenced ambiance of the place as if it was still in the early 1950s.

After the waiter left, he continued. "Let me give you some examples. My old commanding general, when I was with the 25th Division just a few miles northwest of Saigon, was one of the worst military leaders we had. General Van Nguyen Hoa was accused of selling rice to the Viet Cong. He sold food that was supposed to be for our troops, and military equipment too."

He took a sip of tea because his throat was getting dry from all the talking he was doing.

"Just go to the Dan Sinh market in Cholon sometime and see all the helmets, boots, field equipment, guns and ammo that should be in Army storage facilities instead of there. It was all government property, supplied to us by the Americans, and then sold on the black market by our generals." He paused to let Henri think that over.

Henri nodded in understanding and said, "I've been there before and once bought some binoculars from one of the market vendors. I thought that stuff had been scavenged from battlefields. I had no idea it was sold straight from military supply warehouses by the generals in charge," he whispered with a high-pitched tone of surprise. "That's outrageous!"

"That's only part of the problem. General Hoa even sells deferments from duty."

"What does that mean?"

"A soldier would pay the general a fee and then he could leave his unit and maybe get a job working on an American base for much higher wages than he was earning as a soldier. Some of them returned to their units and some never did."

Nha stopped just long enough for another quick sip of tea and a look around the room to see if anyone was trying to eavesdrop.

"General Hoa also made money by padding the division payrolls with phantom soldiers, putting the pay of soldiers that didn't exist into his own private bank account."

"You mean like make up some names or leave the names of dead soldiers on the payroll?" Henri asked, with raised eyebrows and a tone of surprise in his voice.

"Both, and that sometimes caused problems with their bosses higher up in their chain of command," Nha explained.

"How so?"

"Because their forces were thought to be much stronger numerically than they actually were. For example, the Corps Commander might think that the 25th Division had 10,000 men, but because the Division Commander had sold so many duty deferments, and counting deserters, and a padded payroll, the division might actually be at only half-strength. Then when they got into a big battle, they would get their ass kicked by a larger and stronger enemy force because they were an under-strength and weaker fighting unit to begin with."

"I had no idea things like that were going on," declared Henri, visibly shaken by Nha's revelations.

"It's much worse than that, believe me. General Duong Pham Diem of the 5th Division, which is just a few miles directly north of Saigon, has been doing the same thing. And those two divisions, guarding Saigon's northern approaches, are supposed to be two of the strongest elite divisions we have. So imagine, if those two divisions are just hollow shells of what they are supposed to be, at around fifty percent of their reported strength, with less food and supplies than they are supposed to have because of their commanding general's greed, what is the rest of the Army like? The same, maybe even worse, and the enemy knows it!" Nha virtually hissed through his teeth, his anger clearly showing now as he tried his best to remain calm.

"The next thing that weakens the government is something I call 'the numbers game.' Our generals tell the American generals that our military forces are stronger than they actually are. They show them numbers that are false and meaningless, only trying to impress the Americans and make them believe that they are capable leaders, which is just the opposite of what they really are. They falsely raise the numbers of enemy killed also, just like some American units do with their 'body count' statistics. American advisors tell their generals that Vietnamese units are better than they actually are so they don't look bad in the eyes of their superiors. That, in turn, gets reported to the American politicians. Their president actually believes the Vietnamization Program is going well because of all those inflated numbers and so they speed up the departure of all their combat units."

Nha paused to take another quick look around the room and to give Henri a chance to think about what he'd just said.

"South Vietnam is now like an egg whose yolk has been drained out through a hole in the bottom of the shell. Before you know it, all that's left is an easily crushed empty shell that represents our true fighting capabilities and the Communists know that. Add those facts together with the wide-spread corruption that plagues our political leaders and their political appointees in high government offices and many generals and the whole country is ready to collapse, as easily as an empty egg shell."

Henri just sat there, stunned. It was a full minute after Nha finished with his version of how he saw things before he was able to say anything.

"So you believe the government won't last long after the Americans leave?"

"You're starting to repeat yourself, my friend. Yes, that's what I've been told and I've found no reason not to believe it. Like a sandcastle built on the beach, when the high tide comes in, our forces will be swept away by the waves of Communist forces and the Americans won't be around to help. When that day comes, it will be every man for himself. Our president, along with many top politicians and generals have been putting their ill-gotten fortunes in foreign banks and buying investment properties overseas for years. I suspect it's because they know the end is coming too. When the ship begins to sink, the rats will be the first ones off to seek shelter elsewhere. But, before that happens, I hope to send some of those rats to prison. Then they'll be forced to go down with the ship, as they say."

Nha finished the last of his tea and sat quietly.

"I wish it was not so, but I guess you

know more about what's going on than I do. Thank you for sharing that information and your thoughts with me," Henri whispered back across the table.

Nha was finished with his lengthly explanations and acknowledged Henri's last comment with a nod of his head. He then excused himself, got up from the table quietly and disappeared into the crowd that was walking past the restaurant.

Dieu vous garde mon ami. Henri sat for another minute after Nha left and finished his tea. He was still having a hard time believing everything he'd just heard. If it was all true, then my life has just gone from bad to worse, much, much worse. And what of Genevieve? Sacre bleu!

CHAPTER 7

First Lieutenant Tom Ross, U.S. Air Force, was sitting on a bar stool at Mimi's, one of many neon-lit nightclubs on Tu Do Street in Saigon. This was his third stop already and it might not be the last. He'd already been to Club Tiger and Moulin Rouge. He hadn't seen very many Americans in either place so he decided to move on.

You could always tell from the outside if there were many customers on the inside. Bar girls would often congregate at the door of a nearly empty establishment and try to lure in customers with empty promises of a good time or by telling GIs walking by on the sidewalk, how much they loved them. Most of the girls spoke only a very limited amount of English and stuck to a few basic sentences like, "I love you beau coup. Come here, GI. Buy me drink, I show you good time!"

Ross was not here to have a good time though. He was on an intelligence-gathering mission and Mimi's looked like a target-rich environment. It was a well-known fact that GIs who drank a lot, had a tendancy to talk a lot too. He hoped to use that to his advantage. The dimly lit interior of Mimi's held a good crowd of off-duty GIs this evening, just what Ross was hoping for.

Captain Daniels had told him during his in-processing at the 1st SIU, that he was going to get the chance to free-lance and be on his own for awhile. The air traffic in and out of Tan Son Nhut had decreased over the past month and that was why he wasn't going to take the place of the other Air Force officer who'd gone home on emergency leave. It was felt that the remaining three members of the team assigned to the air base could handle the present workload.

Ross was OK with that. The only thing that worried him about free-lancing was the lack of a partner to watch his back in this dangerous environment. Most GIs who went into downtown Saigon or anywhere else for that matter, were encouraged to use the buddy system, with two or more people watching out for eachother. The .38 caliber revolver he carried in his right boot was his "buddy" for the time being. He hoped he wouldn't have to use it.

Saigon was a big crowded city with a growing crime problem. The population had swelled over the years because of people fleeing from areas where heavy fighting had taken place. Many deserters from the South Vietnamese armed forces were scattered throughout the city, being some of those who had fled from the fighting. Some of them went to work at honest jobs, but many of them joined gangs and found ways to make money from extortion, theft and dealing in drugs or prostitution.

Unfortunately, a portion of Saigon's growing population was made up of hundreds of young Vietnamese men who had been medically discharged from military service due to the loss of an arm or leg or two. Several of these armless or legless veterans could be seen every day just outside of the Tan Son Nhut Air Base gates, begging for money. Sadly, their futures looked as dim as their country's.

Duong Tu Do, meaning Freedom Street in English, was known to GIs as Tu Do Street. It was the location of a variety of different types of businesses like bars, restaurants and discos. They were frequented by many Americans before military authorities put a lot of those establishments off-limits.

There were some places where GIs could go, without having to shoo away pesky bar girls, beggars or drug peddlers. At one end of Tu Do Street was a beautiful Catholic cathedral and not far from that was the Vietnamese president's executive mansion, named Independence Palace. Those two points of interest always had a few tourists around, snapping photos or buying picturesque postcards from sidewalk vendors. There were usually a few police around those landmarks as well, so it was a relatively safer area to be in, relatively being the key word.

Ross was slowly sipping a rum and coke, light on the rum, heavy on the coke. He intended on staying sharp and not let his guard down. It was a warm and muggy night and the window air conditioners were having a hard time keeping the interior of Mimi's cool. A large crowd of smokers kept the air tinted a smokey blue and the noise level up as they increased the volume of their conversations to be heard over others who were doing the same. Nobody had put a dime in the jukebox in a while, so at least their voices didn't have to compete with loud music.

After the sun went down in the city, the humidity level never seemed to go down with it and Ross had sweat trickling down his lower back as evidence. As he looked around the crowded nightclub, he noticed that almost half of the guys here had a bar girl either standing or sitting next to them. In a few instances, some bar girls were sitting on the laps of some of the patrons. There was going to be a lot of Saigon tea sold here tonight, he thought, and probably more than that. He had already turned down a couple of "you buy me tea" requests.

The GI to his right had his back turned, talking to another GI two seats further down. Unlike Ross, they were both wearing jungle fatigues and they were both Army officers. The one with his back turned and doing most of the talking, was a captain. The guy he was talking to was a first lieutenant. They had already downed a few beers and Ross hoped to pick up on some good information, so he listened in.

The Army captain wore a West Point Military Academy class ring. He was boasting to the first lieutenant about how he got his Distinguished Flying Cross (DFC). He'd been an advisor to a South Vietnamese Ranger Battalion. The Vietnamese called their American military advisors "co-van," a term that meant "trusted friend."

The captain told the lieutenant that he had a friend who piloted a single engine O-1 Birddog spotter plane. Most of the time his friend and an artillery liason officer who flew in the back seat with him, would call in artillery strikes and fighter bomber support to assist Vietnamese and American combat troops in contact with the enemy.

One day, the artillery liason officer was too sick to fly. The pilot was scheduled to do a bomb damage assessment (BDA) of an Arc Light mission. Three B-52 bombers were going to turn a piece of real estate into moon craters and trees into toothpicks and maybe even kill a few enemy troops in the process. Since the back seater's job for that particular mission wouldn't require any of the skills of a regular artillery liason officer, his friend offered him a chance to do something unique that day. The captain jumped at the chance.

As Ross listened to the story, he wondered if it would include things like acts of bravery, near-death experiences, or something way out of the ordinary. In any case, he was curious enough now that he decided to stick around for a few more minutes and find out.

The two Army officers lit up white-tipped cigarillos, ordered another beer and then the captain continued on with his story. He told his drinking buddy that he and his pilot friend flew at a safe distance from the target area when the B-52s unloaded tons of bombs on it. Then after the smoke and dust cleared, they flew low over the devastated area to complete the BDA.

Extolling the virtues of ticket-punching as a means of career advancement, the slightly buzzed captain then told the lieutenant that after the mission, he returned to his duties as an advisor. He wrote himself up for a DFC, got his Vietnamese unit's commander to write an endorsement since the B-52 mission was flown in support of his unit, and then got a friend who worked in Admin to endorse it and put it in the system.

When the story-telling captain paused to take another drink, the wide-eyed lieutenant asked him incredulously, "You put yourself in for it and it got approved?"

"Hell yeah it did!" he replied, with a big "I told you so" grin.

"Sierra Hotel!" the lieutenant declared, slightly slurring the first word and belching after the second one.

"But that's not all, young buck, there's more! I'm only six months into my tour and I've already got a DFC, a Republic of Vietnam Campaign Medal with two oak leaf clusters, a Republic of Vietnam Galantry Cross with palm and a Vietnam Service Medal with one oak leaf cluster. My six month assignment as an advisor to a South Vietnamese Ranger unit is over. Now I'm gettin' my ticket punched as an aide-de-camp to a general at USARV (United States Army Republic of Vietnam) HQ at Long Binh. How's that for moving up?" the bragging captain asked.

"Sierra Hotel!" the lieutenant replied once again, with a big grin and eyes that now looked a little unfocused.

He held his beer bottle up high in the direction of the captain he now admired and said, "I'll drink to that!"

The captain tapped his beer bottle up against the lieutenant's in a toast and said, "Hell yeah!" once again.

Ross reflected on the captain's story for a moment and then quickly lost any respect he may have had for the former advisor. If that is what it takes to be a successful career Army officer, then Lord, help us, he thought.

The only thing he'd heard so far this evening that was worth checking on was about a drugstore on Tu Do Street. It was near Mimi's so he'd go there next.

One of the customers had walked up to the bar on his left and ordered a Screwdriver. When the bartender served it to him, the guy leaned over the bar and asked him if he knew where he could get something to help him stay awake all night. After the customer returned to the table where he and three other GIs were playing cards, he apparently told his buddies about the drugstore that was nearby. As soon as they all finished their drinks, they got up and left.

Ross decided to follow them, staying far enough behind so that they wouldn't feel like they were being tailed. He was glad to be out of Mimi's. He didn't smoke on a regular basis and the place was so full of tobacco smoke that he was looking forward to getting into some cleaner air. Saigon didn't have any clean air to speak of, cleaner being a relative term in this case.

On a daily basis, the heavy city traffic included thousands of mopeds and motorcycles that burned an oil and gas mixture that resulted in a blue exhaust. There were hundreds of busses and trucks that burned diesel fuel, also adding to the dark exhaust in the air, not to mention the odors. The outside air sometimes looked almost as blue from engine exhaust smoke as Mimi's did from tobacco smoke.

As Ross approached the well-lit entrance to the drugstore the group had entered ahead of him, they walked out and headed back towards Mimi's. He heard one of them say, "This shit is so cheap, I can't believe it!"

Then one of his buddies chimed in with, "That place puts the drugs in drugstore, ha, ha!"

They all laughed over that comment and soon they were too far away for him to understand what else was said.

None of them looked like they were old enough to vote or legally buy a beer back in the States. Yet, here they were, four off-duty soldiers, old enough to fight and die for their country. Knowing that each day might be their last, these pimply-faced teens were playing fast and loose with their money and their health. They were some of the last remaining pawns on the chessboard controlled by the politicians in D.C. Whether or not they would still be on the board at the end of the game was not within their control. Some understood that and some didn't.

Ross decided to tell Captain Daniels about this drug-selling drugstore tomorrow. It would be his CO's call as to what to do about it. He turned away from it and almost bumped into a small Vietnamese man who'd walked quietly up behind him on the sidewalk. He just about jumped out of his skin.

The man wore a tan trench coat over his regular clothes and a gray fedora that looked like something Clark Kent wore in the old 1950s Superman TV show. He opened both sides of the unfastened coat wide enough to show off many knives fastened to both sides.

"You buy knife?" he asked.

"No, thanks," Ross replied, while shaking his head no.

The little man let go of the sides of the coat and quickly rolled up his left sleeve, revealing his arm that was lined with different styles and brands of wristwatches. They covered his arm from his wrist to his elbow.

"You buy watch?" he asked.

"No, thanks," Ross replied again.

Letting go of his left coat sleeve, the man then reached into his left coat pocket and brought out a small plastic bag of marijuana.

"You buy drugs?" the small man asked, with a pleading look in his eyes.

Ross quickly looked to his left and right, thinking, where's a cop when you need one? He was ready to call it a night and catch a cab back to his billet on Cong Ly Boulevard.

He remembered some of the Vietnamese phrases he'd learned since he arrived and told the pint-sized salesman, "Di di mau!" meaning, go away quickly!

Right after he said that, he heard some police sirens approaching from up the street.

Apparently the little peddler did too and he ambled off in the direction of a nearby side street. What was he going to ask me to buy next, his sister? Ross asked himself sarcastically.

Just then, a blue and yellow taxi pulled up, the driver having seen his waving arm. As he got in, two jeeps sped by with lights and sirens going. One carried three Quan Canh, Vietnamese military police, with big white letters "QC" on the front of their dark green helmets. They were members of the 3rd Quan Canh Battalion, garrisoned in Saigon. The other jeep held four members of the U.S. Army's 716th Military Police Battalion, also assigned to Saigon. Both jeeps had M-60 machine guns mounted on a metal post at midframe.

As Ross twisted around in his seat in the back of the French-made taxi to see where the jeeps were headed, they stopped right in front of Mimi's. Looks like I left that place just in time, he thought.

He'd just entered his room on the second floor of the building used to house U.S. military members in downtown Saigon. This billet was for officers only. Just as he was locking his door, he heard some giggling out in the hall. It sounded like a young girl to him and to his knowledge, there were no females assigned to any rooms in the building. His curiosity got the best of him and he decided to take a peek in the hall.

He looked to his left where the sounds had come from and saw his neighbor and a petite-sized young female enter the room. A lot of Vietnamese women were shorter than American women the same age and looked younger too and he wasn't a very good judge of age to begin with. This girl could have been anywhere between 13 and 23 because he only got a split-second glance, not seeing enough of her face to tell if she was good looking or not. He did manage to see enough of her shapely legs thanks to her short mini-skirt. Nice!

After a quick shower and a change into boxer shorts, Ross lay on his bed watching a couple of geckos near the top of the wall that separated his room and the neighbor that had company. These light green, three-inch-long tropical lizards could walk across the ceiling and not fall as they chased after a meal of insects. Some of them made sounds that seemed like they were saying, "F-you!" He continued to watch them, amazed at their ability to crawl straight up the wall or across the ceiling and never fall.

A few minutes later he turned off his light, deciding it was time to sleep. His neighbor had other ideas. Sounds of squeaking bed springs and female moaning sounds made their way through the thin wall and caused Ross to see images in his mind as to what was going on next door. That didn't help him fall asleep any quicker.

He thought of a sign he'd seen on TV, held up high by a college anti-war protestor at a rally back in the States. MAKE LOVE, NOT WAR, it had said. His neighbor must have seen it too and decided to do something about it.

After considering the possibilities of bringing home a young woman himself for some female companionship, he finally curled his pillow around his head, turned away from that side of the room and tried counting backwards from 100. He timed each number with each moan or groan he could still hear through the wall and his pillow. The countdown lasted quite a while until he finally fell asleep late that restless night.

CHAPTER 8

Not counting the latest bad news, fate had previously struck two blows against Henri Ferrand. The first was when he and his wife, Kieu, had a daughter but no son. In Vietnamese society, a family without male heirs is thought to have come to an end. The purpose of marriage was to continue the family line and parents played an important role in matchmaking. Henri had planned on allowing Kieu to be in charge of that parental responsibility.

For parents with a son, they would seek the assistance of a "go-between" to search for a girl who was skillful at housework and someone who they believed would be a good mother to many children.

Beauty was not as desirable as good character in traditional Vietnamese society. In fact, it was sometimes considered a disadvantage because of the belief that fate was seldom kind to beautiful women. For Henri, that was strike two. Genevieve had grown into a very beautiful woman.

The traditional position of women was totally subordinate to men and their social life was limited. Even if their parents allowed them to attend a movie or theatrical play with a male companion, they had to have a chaperone with them.

Over time, with more interracial marriages between French and Vietnamese and then Americans and Vietnamese, some of the traditional customs of Vietnam were being modified. After Genevieve's Vietnamese mother had died, Henri had given her his blessings to choose her own marriage partner when she got older. He also assisted her financially when she decided to pursue a career and start her own business, something her mother had done many years ago.

Now, having graduated from a private Catholic school that had provided her with an excellent education, Genevieve was now operating her own tour guide business. She could speak English, French and Vietnamese fluently. That was a big asset in that type of profession.

Genevieve Ferrand had her mother's dark brown eyes and black hair. She wore her hair long and straight, down to her waist as her mother had done. She wasn't quite as slender or small-boned as her mother, who had been only five feet tall. She had grown to five feet four inches and weighed one hundred five pounds. Her figure had more curves than the average Vietnamese female due to her father's French genes. She also had a lighter skin tone and slightly thinner nose than her mother. She was a beautiful mix of Asian and European ancestry.

When out in public, she wore the traditional Vietnamese ao dai, consisting of long black silk pants under a long sleeve white tunic, slit from hem to waist. At home or with non-Vietnamese friends at leisure, she'd wear a blouse of light or medium gray with her black pants, always dressing very conservatively, even during the Tet holiday.

Tet Nguyen Dan is the full name of the lunar new year holiday commonly referred to as Tet. The Vietnamese New Year is observed during the first several days of the lunar calendar beginning at the second new moon after the winter solstice. That puts it either near the end of January or early February, rarely the same days each year.

It's totally unlike the New Year celebrated by most other countries on January 1st each year. In the United States, the place where the lunar new year is celebrated even close to the same way as it is in Vietnam is in San Francisco's China Town district. Most Americans refer to it as Chinese New Year there.

In Vietnam, Tet is observed boisterously by some, with parades of giant dragons snaking down the streets, fireworks and parties. Others observe it quietly by staying at home and lighting incense sticks in front of framed pictures of deceased loved ones. They place a cup of tea and a small plate of food, usually banh chung, the New Year's cake, in front of the picture with the incense sticks on both sides in the belief that the spirit of the deceased will share in the observance of Tet by drinking and eating with their living relatives. It's a way for the living to let the deceased know that they have not been forgotten.

Tet marks the beginning of Spring and all work usually stops for the first three days and most shops are closed then. Genevieve had to plan carefully so that she would schedule tours around, and not during Tet. All of Saigon's museums, the zoo, and other points of interest would be closed during that time. She always spent time with her father during Tet since his business was also closed for the holiday.

On some of her holiday visits with him, she would tease him about his reluctance to embrace the Vietnamese beliefs that her mother had taught her when she was a child. For example, Vietnamese tradition puts a lot of importance on the first visitor of the new year to their home.

Her father laughed at the idea, calling it a superstition. "How in the world could the first visitor to your home influence the happiness or well-being of the family during the whole year?" he scoffed. He never made fun of their beliefs per se, he just said this when someone tried to convince him to believe in these things too, which wasn't very often.

Vietnamese believed that if a wealthy man or one with lots of children or one of high social position was the first person to visit you, then the family's fortunes would be correspondingly affected. Because of that belief, some families would go out of their way to invite a special guest to their house, one who met at least one of those criteria.

Genevieve was going to try once again to get her father to eat a banh chung, the traditional New Year's cake, with her this year. For the past several years, she had tried to convince him that eating a banh chung would be another means of insuring prosperity. He had told her before that if he ate one, then he would be admitting that he believed in that Vietnamese superstition, and therefore wasn't going to eat any. What a hard-headed Frenchman he was.

A group of six Australians, three doctors

and three nurses, were the last tourists that
Genevieve was taking on a tour of Saigon before the start of the Tet holiday. They were
all members of their army's medical corps and
had completed their tours of duty. Now they
just wanted to relax and see the side of Vietnam they hadn't seen before. Until now, they
had only seen the war-torn side of it. They
weren't scheduled to fly home for a couple of
days so they decided to shop for some souvineers and take some pictures while they went
sightseeing to pass the time.

The tour began with a trip south of downtown Saigon, traveling in a small bus down
Trieu Quang Phuc, one of Cholon's busiest and
noisiest streets. The morning air was already heating up, another bright sunny day
with only a few whispy white cirrus clouds.
They were too thin and too high to cast any
shadows on anything the tourists might choose
to photograph. The only thing that took away
from the beauty of the day was the dark cloud
of smelly diesel exhaust the old rented tour
bus spewed out.

Their first stop was on Le Loi Boulevard,
near the main entrance to the Ben Thanh market. This was no ordinary market. The
French had built the main structure in 1914,
made of reinforced concrete. It was a very
large, very French, piece of architecture,
with a massive clock tower. They called it
Les Halles Centrales, Central Market Halls.
The Australians were amazed at not only the
architectural design and size of the market
but at the diversity of the items the hundreds of vendors offered for sale.

Genevieve talked them into trying some
banh chung that were now being sold as a
specialty item, available only once a year.
The vendor they bought the cakes from made
theirs from glutinous rice, mung bean paste

and fatty pork, wrapped in banana leaves and tied into small, almost square bundles with strips of bamboo to hold them together as they were boiled. Most of the doctors and nurses in her group described the taste diplomatically as "interesting." She enjoyed the free one she got for bringing the vendor more business.

The tour group then headed for Duong Tu Do, meaning Freedom Street. Most westerners just called it Tu Do Street. They stopped at Independence Palace first, then Queen of Peace Church, where some American GIs stationed in Saigon got married, Genevieve told the group.

From there they toured the very picturesque Notre Dame Basilica. It was a red brick cathedral, built by the French. Most notable were its twin spires and many group photos were taken there with Genevieve doing most of the picture taking for the group poses.

After that, they traveled to an area of Saigon that Genevieve called Embassy Row. Their bus stopped near the corner of Thong Nhut Boulevard and Mac Dinh Chi Street. Thong Nhut means "unification" and from their vantage point, they could see the British Embassy and the American Embassy since they were across the street from one another. The French Embassy was on the south side of the U.S. Embassy. They were now about half-way between the zoo at the north end of Thong Nhut Boulevard and the Vietnamese Prime Minister's office at the south end.

Because of tighter security precautions taken after the Viet Cong attack against the U.S. Embassy during the 1968 Tet Offensive, their tour bus wasn't allowed to park any closer than the spot they now occupied. They still managed to take a few pictures of the building that was shown on the evening news so often only four years prior, without leaving the shade of their bus. It was now close to noon and the heat and humidity were both climbing towards their peak.

Genevieve told the Australian tourists that they were going to take a break and get something to eat before continuing on with the rest of the tour. They all commented in favor of that. They still had to visit the Vinh Nghiem Pagoda and the zoo before the tour was over and everyone was ready for a meal and a cold drink.

They were in for a pleasant surprise. Genevieve told the driver to take them to The Kangaroo Club, an Australian-themed pub that served cold beer and hot barbeque. Their menu included just about anything that could be cooked over hot coals on a bamboo skewer with a side order of rice. That included shrimp, dried squid, fresh water eel, goat, water buffalo, pork, chicken, or for the real connoisseur of Asian delicacies, dog du jour.

The tour bus pulled up to the curb near the club.

"Make sure you take everything with you when you get off the bus," Genevieve instructed. It went without saying that thieves would steal anything that wasn't nailed down.

Then she got out of the bus and waited on the sidewalk as the others gathered up their belongings. A couple of the doctors pointed up at the sign over the club that had a hand-painted cartoonish-looking yellow kangaroo wearing red boxing gloves that was the club's trademark. When the rest of the group noticed it, they all chuckled and commented about it. Everyone's hands were full with cameras, souvineers, handbags and things as they headed towards the entrance of The Kangaroo Club.

Walking down the same sidewalk from the opposite direction was First Lieutenant Tom Ross. He was wearing his favorite uniform of the day, a tan short sleeve polo shirt, slightly faded blue jeans, a wide leather belt and boots. He was headed for a bank just a few buildings past The Kangaroo Club.

He was running low on Piasters and needed to change a few dollars of Military Payment Certificates, commonly called MPC or funny-money by a lot of GIs. He knew the conversion rate was higher if he dealt with a black market money changer in the street but he didn't want to take the chance of being cheated by an unscrupulous money-changing con man with fast hands or get caught by undercover cops, which would be very embarrassing since he was working undercover in a law enforcement role himself. There were some things that he was willing to take risks on but this was not one of them. He'd just have to be satisfied getting the official rate of two hundred fifty Piasters to the dollar instead of the three hundred or more a person could get.

As Ross walked towards the bank, he saw a group of people getting out of a small bus. They were walking towards him and he noticed that a motorscooter with two male riders was slowing down as it headed towards him also. A Vietnamese woman in an ao dai was pointing towards a club and the others, all carrying a lot of miscelaneous stuff, were going towards the business she was pointing at. Another Vietnamese woman was holding the door of the place open, gesturing to those on the sidewalk to enter. He slowed his pace down a little, hoping the group would not be blocking his path on the sidewalk by the time he got to the place they were at now. He'd arrive there in a matter of seconds.

The driver of the motorscooter coasted it over to the side of the road right up to the curb, approaching the group from the rear. They neither heard nor noticed it. Suddenly, in the blink of an eye, the passenger, slightly smaller and younger-looking than the driver, took one step onto the sidewalk and grabbed the shoulder bag that was hanging from the left shoulder of the woman in the ao dai.

Ross immediately realized what was going on. He instinctively ran towards the motorscooter, an old gray French-built Solex model that had the engine mounted over the front tire.

He waved his arms over his head yelling, "Dung lai! Dung lai!" Stop! Stop!

The driver said something to his passenger and just as the woman was turning around in response to the snatching of her shoulder bag, she was given a big shove. Her tour group and bus driver were in no position to come to her aid and hadn't even seen what happened. Some of them only turned their heads back towards the street after hearing a voice yelling "Dung lai!"

The shove given to Genevieve was the perfect diversion. Instead of pursuing her assailants, Ross literally dove towards her. Years of playing baseball in Oklahoma as a kid and sliding into bases, something he was really good at, was the way he tried to save her from a hard impact with the sidewalk. He didn't have any time to think about it, he just did it, like a knee-jerk reaction. He skidded feet first, landing under the young woman just as she was about to hit the rough, hot pavement. She landed in a heap on his upper thighs and lower abdomen for the most part, which cushioned her fall to a large extent.

Genevieve let out a squeal when she was shoved, knocked off balance and knowing that she was going to get hurt by the fall. All of a sudden she looked down and a man came out of nowhere and she found herself landing on him instead of the sidewalk. Where did he come from? What was he doing down there on the sidewalk? She was shaken and confused, but it was a lot better than slamming down on the hard pavement, that was for sure.

Right after she landed on the stranger, she was helped up by her Vietnamese tour bus driver and one of the Australian doctors. Then the two men helped Ross to his feet.

The driver of the motorscooter gunned the over-worked and under-powered engine, which was straining mightily under the weight of the two male riders. As blue-gray smoke poured from its noisy exhaust, it made its way into traffic. The passenger clutched the woven straw shoulder bag that he'd just snatched, between his stomach and the driver's back.

In Saigon, thieves that rode around in pairs on motorcycles and motorscooters were called "cowboys." It looked like these two cowboys were going to make a clean get-away, until a gunshot rang out. A uniformed policeman was standing in the shadow of an awning only about thirty feet from where Ross and Genevieve had ended up on the sidewalk. Nobody had noticed him in his dark uniform in the shade. He was still pointing his gun at the men on the motorscooter, trying to get off another shot, as the passenger tumbled off the back.

The young thief, still in his teens, was dead before he hit the pavement, striking it hard, like a sack of potatoes falling off the back of a delivery truck. After his limp body hit the street, it rolled a couple of times, ending up near the curb. The shoulder bag he'd just stolen landed right next to him near the puddle of blood that was growing larger by the second.

His partner-in-crime managed to live and steal another day by driving eratically in and out of traffic lanes, too close to other vehicles to give the policeman a clear shot. With its heavy burden cut in half, the motorscooter was finally able to pick up speed, still spewing out blue-gray exhaust smoke from the oil and gas fuel mixture its old engine burned.

Limping slightly, Ross walked over to the shoulder bag in the road and brought it back to the young Vietnamese woman who was now being comforted by the three Australian nurses from her tour group.

"I believe this belongs to you," he said with a smile, as he held out the shoulder bag to her.

He was just now noticing how pretty the young lady was. He was also beginning to notice how much his body hurt, but he still managed to smile through the pain.

"Thank you. Thank you so much for helping me and getting my things back," Genevieve managed to say.

She was still so shook up from what had just happened that she was having a hard time putting her thoughts into words. Never in her life had she experienced something as frightening as being robbed and shoved to the ground and then witnessing someone being shot to death. And never in her life had she met a man so handsome and courageous as to cause her to become both flushed and flustered.

She was still breathing hard but managed

to say, "Please join us inside. You're hurt and these people," as she gestured towards the group of tourists, "are doctors and nurses from Australia and can help you."

"Yes indeed, mate. We're all medical professionals and would be honored to check you over," chimed in the doctor who had helped both he and the woman up from the sidewalk. "Come, let's have a look at you inside where it's cooler. Come along now," he insisted in his Australian-accented English.

The same doctor, who introduced himself as Jeffrey Cunningham, was obviously the ranking person in his group. He instructed the three nurses to give Genevieve a thorough exam, even though she insisted that she wasn't injured at all, just shaken up a little.

Ross, on the other hand, had not been so fortunate. His left elbow and forearm were badly skinned and bleeding a little bit. His left buttock was hurting too but with no visible signs of injury. His denim blue jeans, like his left arm, also showed signs of damage. The friction from sliding on the cement sidewalk left some white gashes in the left rear area, on the pocket and just below it. Their heavy-duty construction kept the skin on his rear end from being scraped but not totally unhurt.

The doctors had his arm cleaned up and bandaged in no time. Ross thanked them and got a "No, thank **you**, mate," in return from the ranking doctor, the spokesperson for the group.

"If you had not intervened when you did, our poor tour guide, Miss Genevieve here," Doctor Cunningham said as he directed a thumb over his shoulder towards her, "could have been seriously hurt, maybe even killed if her head had struck that sidewalk hard enough. You're a bloomin' hero, you are! Who said chivalry is dead?"

One of the other doctors in the group began handing out large, half-liter bottles of ice cold La Rue "Tiger" beer, also known as "B-40" beer to their fighting mates in the bush. They called it that because the brown bottles resembled the B-40 anti-tank rockets used by the North Vietnamese Army. He proposed a toast.

"To our American hero. Without his quick action, we might not be able to finish our tour today and this young lass," pointing his bottle towards the blushing Genevieve, "might not have been so lucky!"

"Here, here!"

"I'll drink to that!"

"You'll drink to anything!"

"Quite right, mate!"

Ross walked over to Genevieve, who had placed her still-full beer bottle on the bar. She had only placed it up to her lips during the toast, not drinking any. She didn't drink alcohol in any form, purely by choice, not because of religious beliefs or anything else. She had joined in the toast merely out of politeness and respect for the beliefs and traditions of others.

The interior of The Kangaroo Club was a lot darker than the sunlit sidewalk outside and Ross wished it was lighter. He wanted a better look at the young woman standing before him. She was dressed in traditional Vietnamese clothing but she didn't appear to be 100% Vietnamese. That intriguing difference and the fact that he found her to be very attractive, caused him to want to learn more about her.

"Are you OK?" he asked.

"Yes, thank you. How badly did you get hurt?" she inquired, having seen his left arm before it was cleaned and bandaged.

"Oh, it's nothing serious. Just some scrapes and bruises. I'll be OK."

Doctor Cunningham walked up to Ross and Genevieve and said, "Excuse me for interrupting, but would you two like to join us for lunch? We've ordered some food, enough for everyone."

"Sounds good to me. How about you, Miss... I'm sorry, I didn't get your name," Ross said, hoping it would be something easy to pronounce and just as easy to remember.

"I am Genevieve Ferrand. May my driver join us too?"

"Why of course, my dear, of course," the tall and elderly Australian doctor enthusiastically replied. "The more, the merrier!"

With that said, he walked back to the tables where the rest of the doctors and nurses sat.

"I'm Tom Ross. Nice to meet you, Genevieve. Shall we join them?"

He was very sore from the slide on the sidewalk and the impact of her body landing on his but he was determined to keep smiling and try to hide the pain.

Genevieve led him to the table where the tour bus driver was sitting and said a few things in Vietnamese to the man whose bus she rented. He nodded an affirmative understanding, his smile even bigger than before. The Australian tourists were paying for their drinks and meals.

Ross got there just in time to pull her chair out for her, trying his best to be a gentleman. Limping from the pain that emanated from his left buttock had caused him to be a little slow on his arrival to the table and he was almost too late in reaching her chair before she sat herself.

She looked up at him and smiled the most beautiful smile that he thought he'd ever seen and said, "Thank you" in the sweetest feminine voice he thought he'd ever heard.

"So, Genevieve, what nationality is your last name, if you don't mind me asking?" It certainly doesn't sound Vietnamese to me, he thought.

"My family name, Ferrand, is French. My mother was Vietnamese and my father is French."

She seemed a bit uncomfortable explaining her heritage to this stranger.

He didn't pick up on the "was" when she spoke of her mother. He was in a state of mind that he wasn't accustomed to. He was still in some pain and felt somewhat starstruck, as if he was in the presence of a celebrity, a very beautiful celebrity. It was a feeling that he'd never experienced before.

A waitress brought over a cup of tea, setting it down in front of Genevieve, along with a plate of barbequed chicken strips on bamboo skewers, a bowl of rice and some chopsticks. She then set the same items in front of Ross and the tour bus driver. Looking around at the other tables, Ross saw that the Australians were receiving the same things.

Before he began eating, Ross asked, "When are you taking another group on a tour? I'd like to go on one since I haven't done any sight-seeing yet."

What he really wanted to see was more of the tour guide, under a different set of circumstances.

"Two weeks from today if I get five or six people that want to go. I have to pay for the use of a bus and driver so I need a group of at least five or six."

"How much does it cost for each person?" he asked.

"Ten dollars MPC or the equivalent in Piasters. That would be two thousand five hundred P."

She handed him a business card from her shoulder bag and said, "The bus leaves from that address at nine in the morning and returns there at four in the afternoon. Bring a camera with you because we go to many picturesque places."

Genevieve then picked up her bowl of rice with her left hand, moved it to her lips, tilting it up slightly and deftly used the chopsticks in her right hand to scoop the rice into her mouth. She wondered if Ross knew how to eat rice with chopsticks.

Most westerners she'd observed, failed miserably and ended up using a fork or spoon. They didn't realize that the bowl had to be lifted from the table to one's lips in order to eat rice properly. She had seen some people fail because they left the bowl on the table and tried to lift a few grains of rice at a time. Most of the rice didn't make it to their mouth. She thought it was so comical as she watched them struggle with their chopsticks.

Ross still had to get some Piasters from the bank down the street and get back to work. He had only finished half of his beer, two of the four barbeque chicken-on-a-sticks, and didn't touch his rice at all. He really needed to get going.

"Well, Genevieve, it was nice meeting you. I've really got to get going now so I'll see you again in two weeks for a tour." *Provided I can either get the day off or somehow make the tour a part of my job*, he thought.

"Thank you so much for helping me today. Nice meeting you too, Mister Ross," she replied, giving him a demure smile.

"Please, call me Tom," he said as he

noticed her shy demeanor. He found it both charming and appealing.

"OK, Tom. Thank you again."

Her smile was having an affect on him and it made him look forward to that tour in two weeks. Oh yeah, he couldn't wait.

He turned to the Australian doctors and nurses at the nearby tables and thanked them for their help, the beer and the meal. He shook all of their hands before leaving the club.

At the end of the day, Ross was back in his billet, replaying the scenes of his encounter with the cowboys, Genevieve, and the Australians. They were going through his mind as if he was a movie producer reviewing the frames of a film, one by one. What had started out as a routine day, ended up being anything but routine. He lay on his bed, staring up at the ceiling.

He saw things in slow motion, starting with the punks on the strange-looking motorscooter. Who puts the engine over the front wheel like that, he wondered? His mind was in instant replay mode as he recounted the passenger grabbing the woman's shoulder bag and giving her a shove. He heard himself yelling for them to stop and saw himself sliding in slow motion as if he was trying to steal second base in a ball game.

He could feel the pain in his left arm as it scraped along the sidewalk. He felt the weight and pressure of the woman as she fell on his legs and stomach. After being helped up, he looked in the direction of the gunshot and watched the young punk slowly fall from the back of the motorscooter, tumbling in slow motion in the road.

He remembered retrieving the woman's

shoulder bag from the side of the road but couldn't remember what he said when he gave it to her.

In the dimly lit club, he could vaguely remember being treated by people with funny accents and eating at a table with a Vietnamese man and a woman who was only half Vietnamese but dressed as if she was 100% Vietnamese. He didn't remember much of what either of them said, only that he'd see her again in two weeks.

He couldn't get that beautiful smiling half-French, half-Vietnamese face out of his mind. It was stuck there, just like a song he heard on the radio right before he left Oklahoma, playing over and over again. He didn't know who called his favorite AM radio station, KOMA, when the request line was open. Whoever it was, they liked the same music that he did and now he couldn't get the events of the day to stop replaying in his mind any more than he could get that song to stop a couple of weeks ago.

The next two weeks couldn't go by fast enough, he thought. The last thing he remembered before he fell asleep was the pretty young woman who had been wearing an ao dai, with not-quite-round, brown eyes, long dark hair and a slender, attractive figure with an infectious smile that brought forth a smile on his own face. And her voice, that soft, sexy, French-accented voice. He couldn't wait to hear it again. It was the last thing he heard as he finally fell asleep that night.

Before he went to breakfast the next morning, Ross got out his shoe-shine kit. His tan boots had gotten scuffed up some by the slide on the sidewalk the day before. He had a lot of things to remind him of what had happened. His sore arm and rear end were constant reminders plus a pair of jeans he had to throw away because of the damage done to them by the rough slide and his tan Western-style boots badly scuffed up on one side. All that for just trying to do the right thing, he thought.

He noticed something else now that he hadn't seen before. His large silver belt buckle had left a red mark on his stomach where it had been violently pressed into him by the weight of the young woman's body when she fell on him. Only the upper half of the belt made contact with his stomach so he had the outline of a half-moon-shaped red mark that sloped downwards at both ends, reminding him of a cattle brand. He was now feeling a little sore there too.

Well, at least she missed the family jewels, he jokingly thought to himself as he began to put a new shine on his boots. Things could have been a lot worse, that's for sure.

CHAPTER 9

John Brenner, Steven Mann and Cecil Decker were not happy campers. They were all members of the Central Intelligence Agency. They had hoped to be assigned to either an Air America detachment or a main office like the one attached to the U.S. embassy in Saigon. Instead, they'd been assigned to a one-of-a-kind joint task force unit commanded by an Army officer. They were not operating in the usual way, that was for sure.

They rented a nice large house on Gia Long Street, about a half mile from the U.S. embassy. One of the first things they did was to become familiar with their new neighborhood and surroundings. About two blocks away from their house was a ten story building that housed the U.S. Agency for International Development (USAID).

The U.S. ambassador lived over on Dien Bien Phu Street, across from a large cemetery that was only four blocks from the embassy. The Marine embassy guards lived in a converted hotel on Hong Thap Tu Street, not far from Gia Long Street. Since they weren't very far from other Americans living in Saigon, the three CIA agents didn't feel totally alienated.

They had just finished their breakfast and two of them were having their second cup of coffee, about to leave their house for another day of work.

"Another day, another dollar," Decker sighed.

At forty two, the married father of two girls was the elder of the trio. His sun-bleached blond hair was starting to show a little gray around his temples.

"Don't you mean, another day, another Piaster?" Brenner asked, putting his own humorous perspective on the old adage.

He was two years younger and two inches shorter than Decker, standing at an even six feet. However, he was at least twenty pounds heavier, tipping the scales at one hundred ninety pounds. His light brown hair showed no signs of graying. He was also married, with one son in elementary school. He had seniority over the other two agents.

There was no come-back from Mann, the twenty-five-year-old "youngster" of the group. He was drinking a cold bottle of orange soda, wondering why the other two guys drank hot coffee on an already hot day. He preferred his $C_8H_{10}N_4O_2$ cold. That was caffeine to the chemistry major who got bored with it and on a whim one day, decided to see what the CIA had to offer. So far he'd found nothing boring at all with his training, the CIA in general or with life in Saigon.

"OK guys, it's time to go act like three off-duty GIs on a 3-day pass again. Let's get crackin'," Brenner said, as he set his empty coffee cup down in the kitchen sink next to Decker's.

Mann's dark brown hair, worn only slightly longer than the others, but still within GI regulations, was already covered by a wide-brimmed boonie hat. He was eager to get started. He reached down to his right ankle and tapped his holstered pistol just to reassure himself it was there.

Decker noticed the move and asked, "You all ready there, cowboy?"

"Absolutely. Let's go! We're burning daylight!"

The two older agents also wore boonie hats and holstered pistols on their ankles. They believed in the old saying, "There's safety in numbers," especially true in Saigon, but in this case it pertained to the number of weapons, not people. The war had caused Saigon to become an over-crowded and more dangerous city than ever before.

So far the agents had only helped put two drug-dealing businesses off-limits to U.S. military personnel. The bigger fish had eluded them so far but they knew it was only a matter of time before they found what they were looking for.

Just like Lieutenant Ross, they too discovered the drugstore on Tu Do Street. It had been supplying GIs with amphetamines and barbiturates, staying in business longer than it should have because its owner had police protection. U.S. military authorities put the store off-limits to GIs. That's all they could do with their limited authority.

That action only changed the direction of the flow of drugs and did nothing to stop it. It was like turning on a water faucet and trying to stop the flow of water by placing your thumb over it without turning it off. The water would spray out in different directions but wouldn't stop coming out of the faucet.

The drugstore could no longer supply drugs **directly** to GIs. It simply supplied the drugs to bar girls and pimps, creating another level of drug peddlers. The flow of drugs was merely diverted and, like a water faucet with a thumb in front of it, continued to flow, but in different directions.

The second drug operation they encountered was also at a business on Tu Do Street. They had learned that a lot of Americans were doing business with an establishment named New York Tailor Shop. It was on the first floor of a two-story building. There was a massage parlor up on the second floor named Magic Fingers. While the man who owned the tailor shop ran a respectable legitimate business, the same couldn't be said about his upstairs neighbor. The CIA agents noticed that a lot of his GI customers and a few of his American civilian customers as well, headed upstairs after doing business with him first.

It only took a single visit to Magic Fingers to discover that the list of things one could buy there went far beyond a full body massage, a hand-job or a short-time. Slicker than a hand full of lotion in motion, the employees were adept at picking pockets and selling a wide variety of drugs. They even operated an old fashioned opium den in one of the back rooms for clientele with lots of time on their hands and a wish to forget all their troubles for awhile.

They also had police protection and continued to operate after U.S. authorities put the "steam and cream" off limits to GIs. There was only so much that U.S. authorities could do as guests in a foreign country.

Headquarters Area Command (HAC) was a service support unit that kept the peace using Army MPs and they assisted staffs, headquarters and offices in and around Saigon in the 50 square mile Capital Military District. After Magic Fingers was put off-limits to all American military personnel, the three agents found out from one of their contacts in HAC that there were now one hundred and eight businesses on the off-limits list. The last two were a result of their diligent work and they intended on adding several more.

They'd been walking for awhile when Mann thought he heard a familiar sound.

"Hold up a minute, guys. Check this out," agent Mann said, as he stopped and pointed down a narrow alley that connected into Tu Do Street.

"What is it?" Brenner asked.

He and Decker stopped and looked down the alley where Mann was pointing.

"Listen. Do you guys hear that?"

"Hear what?" Brenner asked, as he cupped an ear with a hand.

"You mean the sound of a generator?" asked Decker.

Without answering, Mann led them into the narrow sun-lit alley to a point just behind a nightclub that fronted Tu Do Street. A large green generator sat on some wooden four-by-fours and was humming along at normal speed. He looked it over closely and took a small note pad and pen from his pocket and jotted down some numbers he found on a metal plate attached to the generator. On one of the generator's green support beams were the words PROPERTY OF U.S. ARMY, stenciled in black.

Several times a day, rolling brown-outs and black-outs affected neighborhoods all across Saigon. The power grid just couldn't handle the load put on it. Those who could afford one, bought a generator. Others just stole them from the Americans, who seemed to have a lot of everything.

"This is stolen property, no doubt about it," Brenner stated after thoroughly looking over the generator himself.

"You've got good hearing there, cowboy.

Way to go!" Decker commented enthusiastically. "I didn't notice the sound myself because of all the street noise."

They went back out to Tu Do Street and Mann wrote down the name of the bar in his note pad.

Agent Brenner, the team leader, patted Mann on the back and joked, "I may have to switch from coffee to orange soda if you keep this up, ha, ha!"

"Well, at least we're off to a good start today. I'd hate to tell Captain Daniels that we didn't find anything at all to report on," replied the youngest member of the trio.

"You got that right," agreed Brenner.

"Yeah, anything's better than nothing at all," added Decker. "But, let's hope we find more than just that."

They were on a hot streak. Less than an hour later they saw a strange sight as they walked along the sidewalk of another busy street. A large deuce-and-a-half truck turned off the main street into an alley across from where they were walking. Within a few seconds, they had an unrestricted view of the truck, which was piled high with duty-free PX goods. They watched, dumbfounded, as the truck drove slowly down the alley. There was a wire strung across it, only a few inches higher than the cab. As the truck drove along slowly, the wire knocked the top packing cases off it.

As soon as the boxes hit the ground, several men appeared in the alley and carried the boxes into one of the buildings that had a door facing it. The truck reached the next street at the far end of the alley, then the driver gunned the big diesel engine and it was out of sight before the agents had crossed the busy street.

Try as they might, they couldn't determine

which of the three doors facing the alley the goods disappeared into. They were all windowless and locked. The heist had been pulled off right in plain sight, quickly and professionally. All they could do was report what they'd seen, with a general description of the truck, the location of the alley and surrounding buildings. That theft of U.S. government goods was not the last one they saw that day.

After agents Brenner, Mann and Decker tired of walking in that part of the city, they took a taxi over to Le Loi Boulevard. They ate lunch in a small cafe and then walked over to Nguyen Hue Street, Saigon's famous "Street of Flowers." One block west of there they noticed a car wash business. There were several pale yellow and blue taxis lined up to be washed.

As they approached the side of the small building that housed the car wash business office, something caught the eye of agent Brenner that raised his curiosity level.

"Hey guys, you see what I'm seeing?"

An irregation pump, something designed for use on farms, was supplying the water pressure for the car wash.

"Yeah, let's check it out," Decker answered.

Mann wasn't sure what they were talking about. He had no idea what a pump like that was designed for, if that was what they were interested in to begin with.

"Mann, get your pad out and write the serial number and manufacturing information off of that thing right there," Brenner stated as he pointed to the noisy object that had gotten his attention.

As Mann proceeded to write in his pad, an angry looking Vietnamese man walked towards the three Americans. He began speaking very fast and with a loudness and tone that got the other car wash employee's attention.

Brenner started to get a little concerned.

"Let's go, guys. I don't think we're welcome here. It's time to di di," Brenner said, as he put his hands up and made a motion for the approaching hot-headed guy to back off.

It didn't work. The man pulled a switchblade knife out and began waving it menacingly at the three Americans. As if they'd rehearsed the move many times, they all brought out their .38 Specials in a flash. With three gun barrels pointed at his face, the man did a quick about-face and ran into the car wash office as fast as his Ho Chi Minh sandals could carry him.

When the man disappeared into the darkened office, the three CIA agents beat a hasty retreat. They didn't want to start an incident.

"Hey, Brenner."

"Yeah, Mann."

"How do you say, 'Don't bring a knife to a gunfight'in Vietnamese?"

"Ha, ha, very funny. Let's get the hell out of here," Decker said as they picked up the pace.

"Betcha that U.S.-made irregation pump was the property of USAID," Brenner said to the others as they put some more distance between themselves and the boisterous man with the knife.

Decker suggested they take a cab over to Gia Long Street where the U.S. Agency for International Development was located. It was not far from their rented house and they could walk home from there.

"You think that pump was meant for some poor rice farmers down in the Mekong Delta?"

Mann asked.

"More than likely," Brenner replied. "If the taxpayers back home knew about it being stolen and used at a business owner's car wash, they'd be pissed! I know I am!" It showed in his voice.

As the trio neared their destination, Decker, who'd been quiet as they rode across town in the taxi, volunteered a thought out loud.

"You know, I think I've seen more thefts of government property in the short time I've been here than I have in my entire career. It's unbelieveable! At this rate, this will probably be the costliest war in our country's history. Can I get a 'Amen'?"

"Amen!"

"Amen, brother Decker!"

Their taxi pulled up to the USAID building. After reporting their findings about the water pump, they called it a day and walked back to their place. They were hot, tired and disgusted. None of them felt like they'd accomplished much. After a few cold beers, it didn't seem to matter any more. Another day, another dollar.

CHAPTER 10

Mang Binh Hao, owner of Gulf of Lion Shipping Company, was sitting in front of Henri Ferrand's desk, sipping his tea. Henri's secretary had brought them some freshly-made tea shortly after Hao's arrival. Henri had no idea what Hao wanted to see him about this morning. Hao's face never gave away his thoughts, whether they were good or bad. His perpetual smile was good camouflage for the evil that lurked behind it.

After engaging in a little small talk, Hao finally explained the reason behind his visit, in his own round-about way. He'd been looking over the books that contained years of records about the business transactions that Henri was responsible for. A lot of the transactions Hao had a personal hand in were never recorded, at least, not that he was aware of.

Hao had finally come to realize just how good of a branch manager Henri was. He was pleasantly surprised at the increase in profits from one year to the next, all due to Henri's hard work. Henri was good at what he did, real good, and that pleased Hao very much.

"You have been working for this company for long time now, long before I own it. You have gained much experience and wisdom about how things work in this country. The business decisions you have made, were made with much thoughtfulness, intelligence, prudence and good judgement. You are very wise man for doing that and for doing everything I ask you to do too."

Hao paused for a moment, just long enough to take another sip of tea and notice how uncomfortable and ill-at-ease Henri seemed to be.

Hao continued, "Over the twenty five years that you work for this company, you make many business deals which increase our profits every year. A man with all of those qualities of wisdom, experience, intelligence, prudence and good judgement is truely deserving of a big bonus.

He could tell that Henri wasn't expecting all that praise by the confused look on his face.

"Thank you for the compliments, Hao. I've always done my best for this company." Because of your implied threats, he didn't say out loud.

Had it really been twenty five years already? He'd never given it much thought.

Hao stood up and reached into his right suit pocket and took out a large stack of cash. He did the same with the left pocket, each stack containing about a thousand dollars worth of Piasters.

"Here, for you," he said as he put both stacks of bills on Henri's desk. "It is bonus money for your twenty five year anniversary with this company."

There were no personal words of thanks from Hao, just this gift of cash, "chump change" to a man of Hao's vast wealth. At least he had shown his gratitude in some way, and Henri was both surprised and grateful for that.

"Thank you, thank you," Henri managed to stammer, too stunned to think of anything else to say.

He bowed slightly in deference to his boss, surprised at both Hao's generosity, and the complements he'd been given.

"How was your Tet holiday, Henri? Did you go to Vung Tau and spend time with your daughter?"

He knows I did. I've been doing the same thing year after year. I wonder why he is being so nice today?

"I had a good holiday, thank you. Yes, my daughter and I spent some time together and went to Vung Tau. How about you? How was your holiday?" As if I really cared.

"Good, very good. I go visit friend in Singapore. Many Chinese live there and celebrate new year too."

He took a quick look at his expensive watch and announced, "Have to go now, Henri. We talk more later."

Mang Binh Hao left Henri's office quickly, as if he was going to be late for an appointment somewhere. Henri was glad to see him go. With each passing day he wished he'd never heard of him or this business.

He put the money in a desk drawer and then got up and locked his office door. He wanted to make another entry in his journals without anyone knowing they even existed. He also wanted to review all of the information he'd written on people, including Hao. It was decision time. Who would he turn the journals over to?

He wrote his journal entries as if he was telling a story. His sources for the information on the people he'd written about were many. He felt sure that Hao had no idea just how much he really knew about these crooked generals, politicians and businessmen. A wise man? Yes, more than you'll ever know, Hao, he thought, as he opened the first journal and began reviewing the entries that included the following:

Trung Ho Quoch came from a poor family. He had been a career Army officer, with no business experience nor any rich relatives. His wife has no known legal source of income. Neither his nor his wife's name can be found on any document concerned with any business, legal or otherwise. Yet, he and his wife have become filthy rich. How? By stealing hundreds of millions of dollars, much of it from the American government and the rest from his own countrymen. Like the Mafia, those who are involved in government corruption always shield the head man. In this case, the head man is the President of South Vietnam, Trung Ho Quoch.

Ly Than Mai is the President's wife. Her sister is Ling Thi Xuan (technically a half-sister), who is married to the Chinese businessman, Mang Binh Hao. The President's wife and her brother-in-law front the President's multi-million dollar corruption scemes. They are the ones who put large amounts of money into the Quoch bank accounts in Singapore and Switzerland and make the silent partner investments in Taiwan, Guam and Hawaii.

Mrs. Quoch also uses the cover of visiting her children in Europe to bank the ill-gotten money or convert it into jewelry as another money laundering technique. She has one of the best diamond collections in Asia, in both quality and quantity.

The salary of the President of South Vietnam is equivalent to about $650 U.S. dollars per month with additional side benefits of $350 to $450. He owns two homes in Saigon valued at more than $160,000., a riverside home a few miles north of Saigon, a large villa in Switzerland, and plots of land in several South Vietnamese provinces. To have all that, on his income, would have been impossible were it not for his involvement in corruption and drug rackets run by his senior military advisor and various government ministers.

One of Quoch's major sources of revenue is from smuggling things into and out of Vietnam. Scrap metal from the war is a big part of that business. Tons of brass shell casings and other metal scrap from military sources are smuggled out of Vietnam, some of it on ships owned by Mang Binh Hao. The ships are registered in Panama and crewed mostly by South Koreans.

The journal entries about the President and his wife were lengthly. Henri left a couple of blank pages after each person in case he found more information to write about them at a later date. After he transferred information from notes to the journal, he tore the individual notes into tiny scraps and threw them away in trash cans outside of his own building as a security measure. The next journal entry was:

Vo Tien Dung is the President of Air Vietnam, with an office at Tan Son Nhut International Airport in Saigon. He and

Trung Ho Quoch are good friends. That was because his son is married to Quoch's daughter.

Air Vietnam planes fly to a dozen Asian cities from Saigon. The cargo holds of their planes are filled in Singapore, Tokyo and Hong Kong with goods for the Saigon black market. Things like ciggarettes, cognac, electronic goods, bolts of cloth, dinnerware, cosmetics and drugs are typical items smuggled into the country.

People that are known by customs officials to be friends of the President's family meet the Air Vietnam planes at the airport in Saigon. The smuggled goods are then loaded into cars and trucks while customs officers either turn their backs or stand by and watch. They are in on it too. The goods are then driven straight to warehouses and market places around Saigon and Cholon.

The average black market mark-up on prices is between ninety to one hundred percent. Since the money from these sales of smuggled goods is in Vietnamese Piasters, the Quochs and their partners-in-crime turn to Hong Kong, Asia's money market headquarters, to change the Piasters into U.S. dollars, the strongest currency in the world. The dollars are then either sold directly on the black market for a big profit or used to buy more goods to be smuggled into Vietnam.

After having compiled a lot of information on key government officials, generals and businessmen, Henri could see a pattern taking shape. It was like a spider web, with the

President as the spider in the center and everyone else connected to him through the individual strands of the web. The next entry followed after a few blank pages:

> The brothers of General Nguyen Pham Vinh control the Vietnamese Customs Service. It is notorious for its indifference to the large amounts of opium and other smuggled goods arriving on Air Vietnam to be sold on the black market. General Nguyen Pham Vinh is the Prime Minister of South Vietnam.

The next entry made it clear as to the connections between some of the high-ranking government officials and just how wide-spread the practice of corruption was in the Saigon regime:

> The brother-in-law of the Prime Minister is Brigadier General Tran Van Thien, who is also the Mayor of Saigon. He is known as a big-time influence peddler. He demands and receives gratuities for that service. In return for the payments, he lets it be known publicly that he is personal friends of the businessman concerned, usually a businessman of Chinese descent in Cholon, by attending a special function or by giving a large gift of money at a wedding or funeral. He is aware of Mang Binh Hao doing the same thing so he plays the game of "one-upmanship." If Mang Binh Hao gives someone a gift of one thousand Piasters, the Brigadier General/Mayor of Saigon would give someone a gift of one thousand five hundred Piasters, and so on.
> General Thien has a son who is a Captain in the LLDB, Luc Luong Dac Biet,

the Vietnamese Special Forces. His ego is such that he even uses his favorite son to further his own cause. When his son was awarded the Vietnamese Cross of Galantry medal for bravery, he made sure that he was allowed to pin the medal on his son's chest in a ceremony in Saigon, with photos of the occasion on the front page of Chinh Luan, the Vietnamese language newspaper, The Saigon Post, the newspaper published in English and in Saigon's Chinese language newspaper as well.

General Thien is a publicity hound to the extent that, if he couldn't be on the front page of newspapers showing him bestowing personal attention on selected businessmen, then he would use his military rank and position as Mayor of Saigon to conduct military awards ceremonies fit for a king.

Because of his military rank, his civilian position and his Prime Minister brother-in-law, Thien is in an influential position in Saigon. He is able to approve or block virtually any business in this city.

There was an interesting aspect of the "spider web" connection between the people Henri wrote about in his journals. He noticed a lot of family ties. One key person was either a brother-in-law or married to a sister-in-law, cousin, or some relative of another key person. There were several family connections that stood out in his findings. The next entry in his journal was one of the shorter ones, but no less shocking in regards to the corruption activities of a government official:

Khan Le Trang is the Minister of the Economy in the Quoch administration, given that position by the President. He charges commissions for securing contracts for American companies like PA&E, Pacific Architects and Engineers, to work in Vietnam. The companies pass the commissions along to the American government in the form of higher bids for the jobs, the projects being paid for by the U.S. government in the form of aid.

Trang has a bank account in a Taiwan branch of Chase Manhattan Bank. At one point, he had a cash balance of over six million dollars, all gained from the corrupt use of his position in the South Vietnamese government.

Even if a person was mentioned publicly as being corrupt, it didn't seem to make any difference to either the South Vietnamese or U.S. governments. The person in question simply denied the accusations and went on with their lives as if they **couldn't** be held responsible, like the person in Henri's next journal entry:

Lieutenant General Tan Pham Huu is President Quoch's security advisor and senior military aide. He is very wealthy and owns land and companies in Singapore and Malaysia.

An NBC news correspondent working in Saigon has accused him of being the nation's largest drug dealer. On the TV broadcast, "NBC Nightly News," the correspondent said General Huu is the biggest drug pusher in all of South Vietnam. He further alleged that President Quoch and Vice President Hoang are using money from narcotics sales for

their presidential campaign this year.
The American Ambassador never does anything with the information he gets
about the corrupt Vietnamese generals
and government officials.

That was one of the reasons why Henri was
seriously thinking about giving his journals
to Bui Van Nha, the South Vietnamese CIA
agent that had spoken to him recently. When
Nha told him that he wanted to "send some of
those rats to prison," he'd said that with
the conviction of a man who meant what he
said. Henri just had to make sure that Nha
wasn't on Hao's payroll first.
Mang Binh Hao probably knew all of the
people in his journals and that made him
even more dangerous. Henri was running out
of time but he didn't want to die any sooner
than he had to. He'd rather die from a cancerous brain tumor than at the hands of Hao's
band of hired cut-throats any day. Hao was
the second wealthiest man in the country,
right next to the President near the center
of the tangled web of corruption. He could
afford to pay people to do anything he wanted.
The next couple of journal pages were
about the only person, to Henri's knowledge
anyway, who was fired for being **overly** corrupt. He read over this entry again to make
sure it was as complete and legible as he
could make it so that whoever he ended up giving it to, would be able to understand everything. It stated:

General Le Long Quang is so blatantly corrupt that President Quoch
fired him as commander of IV Corps in
the Mekong Delta right after Tet. He
is known to own at least three homes
and villas in Saigon with an estimated

value of close to one million American dollars. His wife controls distribution of beer and soft drinks to the 305,000 South Vietnamese armed forces members in the Delta. He is very wealthy, but not from his military pay. He comes from a good family and has several political connections, the President no longer being one of them.

The investigation into his corrupt activities began when a captured Viet Cong officer told his captors that General Quang had been selling rice to his unit for some time.

During his tenure as Commander of IV Corps, over 5,000 radios and 20,000 rifles and other small arms disappeared from the Army supply stocks under his control. These American-made weapons and radios were suspected of being sold to members of Saigon's black market community, and possibly to the Viet Cong as well.

Three other South Vietnamese Army generals made it into Henri's journals. He had learned about two of them from Bui Van Nha:

General Van Nguyen Hoa of the 25th Division, just a few miles northwest of Saigon and General Duong Pham Diem of the 5th Division, located a few miles directly north of Saigon, were both accused of selling rice to the Viet Cong. They also sold food, military equipment and deferments from duty.

The two generals also made money by padding their division payrolls with phantom soldiers, putting the pay of soldiers that didn't exist, into their private bank accounts. That made their unit's strengths on paper look much bigger than they actually were. Right now they are still in command of their divisions.

Brigadier General Minh Vinh Giang has been a long-time Viet Cong sympathizer. He works within the Joint General Staff and provides valuable military information to the Communists. He is a traitor but still nothing has been done about him.

Henri set that journal aside and then opened the one he'd started first, several years ago. It was full of the dirt he'd dug up on his own boss, Mang Binh Hao:

Mang Binh Hao was born Chinese and then Vietnamized the spelling of his name. He has many legitimate sources of income. He is the second richest man in Vietnam. The President is the richest.

Because he is an extremely rich and influential businessman and is a member of President Quoch's family by marriage, he became the President's silent partner. He has good connections with the wealthy Chinese businessmen in Saigon and Cholon, of which there are many.

He owns the Phuoc Tuy Textile Company. In 1968, the factory was destroyed by American helicopter gunships during the Communist Tet Offensive. Viet Cong soldiers had taken it over and were using it as a command post.

Hao figured out a way to cheat the American government out of a lot of money because of that incident. He went to the Vietnamese Minister of Finance and filed a claim for damages against the U.S. government. The claim amounted to 200 percent of the cost of the textile factory. He got a note from President Quoch, who is a personal friend of his, to accompany the claim in order to put pressure on the American government to pay up. They paid the claim and Mang Binh Hao rebuilt the textile factory with half of the money and put the rest in the bank.

Hao launders his money made from corruption. He buys land in Taiwan by using middlemen, keeping his name clear. He is also a silent-partner in some of Guam's largest building developments and land holdings. He bought several hundred acres of land in Hawaii too.

He is using his shipping and stevedoring companies to help President Quoch smuggle out tons of brass shell casings and other metal scrap from military sources out of the country. His ships are crewed mostly by South Koreans and registered in Panama.

He often takes payment for the scrap metal in person, out at sea, where he meets with the buyers. Then he goes to Taiwan, Hong Kong, Singapore, the Philippines and Guam in order to launder the money.

Vietnamese tax investigators have looked into the tax returns of Hao and his business associates also suspected of illegal business practices. After the main tax office in Saigon was fire bombed and burned to the ground, the police report listed Viet

Cong sabotage as the reason for the attack. Hao arranged for both the destruction of the tax office and the findings of the police report.

Mang Binh Hao has threatened my daughter and I indirectly through insinuations if I didn't go along with things in this shipping business. Since he bought the company in 1965, I've had to ignore the smuggling of scrap metal and drugs and put whatever Hao tells me to in the business records. He is using my good name and reputation as a screen for his illegal activities.

The entries about Hao were in a separate journal from the others. That was because Henri had originally intended to only keep a record of what he found out about Hao. As he found out things about other people, he decided to put them in other journals, never expecting to collect so much information.

He also decided not to write down the names of the people who gave him the information that ended up in his journals. He knew some of their names, others were just people he met in passing and some of the information came from conversations he'd overheard. He felt it best to just leave out any source names that he did have. That way, if his journals were discovered, nobody else would have to fear for their lives as he did now.

Looking through his journal entries made Henri realize two things. First, that the information he'd written about Mang Binh Hao took up more pages than any of the other entries. That made him the biggest crook of all.

Secondly, also with regards to Hao, he agreed with him that maybe he really was very knowledgeable. Not because of his many years in Vietnam and his accomplishments in his job managing the local office of this shipping company. On the contrary. It was because of all the damning information he'd accumulated over the years on so many different military and political leaders. He knew more about things now than he really wanted to.

The question he asked himself again was, can I trust Bui Van Nha with these journals? If not, would it do any good to turn them over to an American CIA agent? What made it hard for him to decide on their disposition was the onset of another bad headache. He'd decide later.

Satisfied with the review of what he'd written, he quickly locked the journals away in their secret hiding place in his desk. He got up to get some cold water from the office refrigerator so he could take some aspirin but made a detour to his office door to unlock it first. He never made it to the refrigerator.

CHAPTER 11

The members of the 1st Special Investigations Unit were called to attention when the general entered their office. He was wearing starched fatigues that were bloused at the top of his shiny corfam jump boots. The six-foot-four, one hundred eighty pound soldier looked to be in as good condition now as he had in Korea twenty years ago when he was a young infantry platoon leader.

The 1st SIU's twelve officers, their support staff and the MACV commander were going to have a meeting. Everyone was in uniform today because of that. Due to the secret nature of the organization, Lieutenant General Albert Christianson, the current MACV commander, decided to hold the meeting in this office instead of the large meeting room adjacent to his own.

The general commanded, "At ease, take your seats, gentlemen," then started the meeting.

"Gentlemen," the general began, "first of all, allow me to congratulate all of you for the hard work you've done. I'd like to say a special thank you to Army First Lieutenant

Jim Mahoney and Air Force First Lieutenant Bill Fisher. Would you two officers please stand up." When the general said that, it came out as an order, not a question.

The two lieutenants were sitting together and as they stood up, the general began clapping his hands. Immediately, everyone else joined in, not quite sure why these two were being singled out.

Even though Captain Daniels had conducted their mission debrief and was very happy with the findings of their investigation, even he was caught off guard by the attention his subordinate officers were being given by the general. Nobody had ever seen the MACV commander look as happy as he did today and they were eager to find out why. The suspense was palpable in all their faces.

"It's not very often that a message from the Joint Chiefs of Staff comes across my desk with good news. Not only has the investigation of corruption within the Army and Air Force Exchange Service (AAFES) brought down some senior NCOs, but a major general as well. To give notice to all employees and managers at all levels in AAFES that illegal activities will not be tolerated, the story about the findings of the investigation is being given to all the major news agencies for use on TV and in newspapers as well."

The general stood quietly for a moment, pausing and looking around the room, smiling at every single face in the small gathering. Soon there was spontaneous clapping and hoorahing and once it quieted down, he continued.

"The bad news is, due to the nature of the SIU's clandestine operations, the credit for this successful investigation is being given to the Air Force's OSI Detachment 5006 at Tan Son Nhut and the Army's 51st CID in Saigon. But don't feel bad, the media doesn't know anything about the people assigned to MACV SOG or what they really do either."

That was followed by a few polite chuckles from those who understood. He paused again to let that news sink in and to allow for some negative-sounding grumbling to take place. If he was in their shoes, he wouldn't take kindly to that news either. In fact, he had been involved in the investigation to a point. When it was brought to his attention that the major general in charge of the military club system in Vietnam refused to permit the two lieutenants from this unit investigate the network of sergeants who illegally profitted from their operation of clubs, they went to their CO and then the three of them came to him. As their commander, he had no choice but to complain to that general's boss in Hawaii.

The MACV commander looked down at the piece of paper on which he'd written some notes. Then he told the group, "I'm going to tell you exactly what your investigation has resulted in, regardless of what might be said on the TV news or printed in the papers. The news media don't get their facts straight half the time anyway," he said with a chuckle.

Most everyone in the room was shaking their heads up and down in agreement with that statement.

"Corruption has been a problem that the Army and Air Force Exchange Service has had to deal with for some time now. AAFES is responsible for managing not only the post and base exchanges, commissary supplies, Class VI liquor stores and movie theaters, but also servicemen's clubs throughout South Vietnam. It was discovered that some NCOs had used extortion and bribery to pocket part of $25 million collected annually from slot machines in those clubs."

He paused again and the smile on his face changed into a stern look. "And this is the part that **really** pissed me off. My personal plane was used by Sergeant Major Vincent Solarski to transport whiskey in and out of the country. He was also found to be skimming illegal profits from the clubs he was in charge of. The final 'straw that broke the camel's back' as the saying goes, came when the Sergeant Major threatened Lieutenant Mahoney when the investigation into his illegal activities was being done. When somebody threatens one of **my** investigators, that's something I just won't tolerate."

He'd put extra emphasis on the word "my" and he knew that meant something to the members of the 1st SIU. Their commander had their backs.

The general looked down at his notes again, focusing his bright blue eyes to make sure he got the facts right before he proceeded with the rest of the information.

"Master Sergeant Elton Johnson was the manager of several clubs too. He was tried and convicted of similar violations. He was fined $20,000 and dishonorably discharged just like the Sergeant Major. One of the scams they both ran also backfired on them. They took kick-backs from talent agents for booking their acts in the clubs they were in charge of. Now they're both being sued in the civilian courts by the agents."

"And last, but certainly not least, the highest ranking person involved in the AAFES investigation was Major General Tyler Carlton. Those senior NCOs I mentioned earlier were in his command. When that general refused to permit the investigation into his club system, it made him look very suspicious and that didn't sit well with some folks in Washington. The Senate Permanent Subcommittee on Investigations of Government Operations," he read from his notes, "criticized him for inadequate supervision of the club system. The only reason he wasn't sent to Leavenworth, Kansas and brought to trial was because he decided to retire. Normally when a general officer retires, they receive a Distinguished Service Medal. It's sort of the government's way of saying 'thanks' for many years of service, not for a specific achievement. Well, this man so disgraced himself and the U.S. Army, that his DSM was revoked, because of the investigation that I'm proud to say was conducted by Lieutenants Mahoney and Fisher. So let's give them a hand for a job well done. Way to go, guys!"

    The general pocketed his notes and led in the applause that soon filled the room. It was a proud moment indeed and everyone was smiling and feeling good about themselves and about their commanding general who'd shown them his total support in their efforts. The two lieutenants received a few pats on the back and handshakes from other members of their unit.

    After a couple of minutes, General Christianson waved his right hand back and forth over his head to get everyone's attention and it didn't take long for him to get it. He knew that magicians weren't the only people who could make things disappear with the wave of a hand. The noise was gone in an instant.

    "I have one more announcement to make and then I'll let you get back to work." He took out his notes once more and looked over the names and information he was about to address.

    "Would Navy Lieutenant Joe Wagner, Army Captain Larry Johnson and Air Force Captain Barry Westbrook please stand up."

    The three men had been sitting next to eachother on the hard, gray, metal folding chairs used for these large group meetings. They were the team of investigators that had been assigned to Tan Son Nhut Air Base, trying to find any military aircraft and air crew members that may have been involved in smuggling drugs in and out of the country. They had an idea about what was to come next as they stood up to be recognized.

"Gentlemen, I commend you. As a result of your diligent investigative efforts, the command pilot for the American Ambassador to South Vietnam, is now in Federal prison at Leavenworth, Kansas. He was courtmartialed for trying to smuggle approximately $7 million worth of heroin in his aircraft. I'm sure if the ambassador knew specifically who to thank, he would be with me here today. But, as I mentioned before, to be the most effective investigative unit possible, we have to remain unknown because of information leaks that have proven to be problematic to existing agencies. Again, thank you for a job well done!"

The general stuck his notes into his pocket again and began applauding the three officers and everyone else joined in. The three investigators also received congratulatory pats on the back and handshakes from their peers.

General Christianson stepped over to Captain Daniels and thanked him as well, telling him that he had to return to his office to take care of some other matters.

"Room, ten-hut!" Captain Daniels announced loudly.

Dozens of gray metal folding chairs suddenly became empty as everyone stood smartly at attention when the MACV commander strolled out of the room, followed by his adjutant.

A few seconds later, Captain Daniels thanked everyone and then gave the order, "Dismissed!" Time to get back to work.

One of the admin sergeants approached the

CO and commented, "I was surprised at how high-ranking some of the people were that the general mentioned. I just couldn't believe it, senior NCOs, a pilot and a major general, holy cow!"

"Well, Sergeant, you've got to remember, the military is just a microcosm of our society. You know, like a slice of pizza. Imagine a whole pizza with pepperoni on it. You slice it up and each piece looks just like all the other pieces. The military is just like one of those individual pieces and the rest of the pizza represents the rest of society."

Captain Daniels paused to see if the sergeant was understanding his analogy before he continued.

"So if those pieces of pepperoni represented the bad guys and each slice had some pepperoni on it, then the military would have some bad guys just like the rest of society," the sergeant said, totally understanding his CO's use of the pizza in his example.

"You got it! People of all ranks and all branches of the military can become too greedy for their own good and in the end, they'll get caught and go to prison just like their civilian counterparts would. It's a damn shame it happens but it does and it's our job to 'weed out' the bad guys."

With that said, Captain Daniels returned to his office with another cup of coffee so he could stay awake and focused on the paperwork that awaited him. The admin sergeant also went back to his desk job, but now he couldn't stop thinking about pepperoni pizza and he was getting hungrier by the minute just thinking about it.

CHAPTER 12

When Ross called the number on Genevieve's business card, she told him that he was the seventh person to sign up for the next tour. Seven was his lucky number. Two more people signed up for the tour after him.

The Tet holiday was over now and life in South Vietnam returned to normal, but still a country at war. The threat of another country-wide Communist Tet Offensive like that of 1968 was over.

Lieutenant Tom Ross was playing civilian tourist, Mr. Ross today, showing up for the tour in the same casual attire he'd worn when he met Genevieve Ferrand for the first time. The only difference was, he had on a new pair of jeans. He remembered to bring along his instamatic camera too.

Genevieve was looking radiant as always in her traditional Vietnamese ao dai, black pants with a white tunic. Her driver and his bus were the same ones Ross remembered from before.

The other eight people on the tour were all young American GIs from different Army units. Some of them wore cut-off blue jean shorts, others wore regular jeans and casual T-shirts. Once they were all on the bus and under way to the first attraction, they engaged in a lot of small talk.

A couple of guys were from the 90th Replacement Battalion at Long Binh. One specialist was from the 3rd Brigade, 1st Cavalry Division (Airmobile). Another soldier said he was assigned to the 196th Infantry Brigade. The private on Ross' left was a member of the 17th U.S. Army Field Hospital. Two of the youngest soldiers had traveled from 30 miles northeast of Saigon. They had been assigned to F Battery, 79th Artillery Battalion at Fire Base Mace. The last member of their group was a member of D Company, 17th Cavalry. He was a helicopter mechanic, working on the OH6 "Loach," light observation helicopter.

Everyone except for Ross had been relieved from duty from their respective units. They were all scheduled to fly out of Tan Son Nhut on a "freedom bird" back to the states within a few days. In GI slang, they were "short," and that term was used quite a bit that day.

"Hey man, I'm so short I can barely see over the top of my boots!" was a typical example.

Just by coincidence, all of the enlisted men on the tour with Ross that day had been drafted. There wasn't a lifer in the group. When they found out Ross was an Air Force officer, one of them quipped, "We won't hold it against you, sir."

They all laughed at that and it didn't bother Ross at all. He laughed right along with them.

Genevieve took them to the same tourist spots in Cholon and Saigon that all of her tours went. The weather was hot and humid with only a few clouds, a great day for taking pictures. The war seemed to be a million miles away.

When they stopped for lunch, Ross ate with Genevieve and her driver. He was glad that she had suggested he try the pho, the traditional Vietnamese noodle soup. He wasn't very good at using chopsticks and was much more at ease using a soup spoon, even though it was the Chinese-style white ceramic one, larger than an American soup spoon.

He watched how graceful she seemed to be as she ate her meal. He couldn't help himself from looking at her often, trying not to stare.

Genevieve's driver noticed Ross looking at her. Then he leaned over and said something to her in a low voice. She put her spoon down, then dabbed her lips with her napkin. She then looked up, directly into the American's eyes.

"Did you wish to speak to me about something, Mr. Ross?"

Oh no. She'd noticed. Time to come clean.

"I was wondering if you would go out with me to dinner tonight?" he asked, with a sheepish look, as if he'd just been caught with his hand in the cookie jar.

There, he asked her, nerves and all. He found that simple question harder to ask than it should have. He didn't know if he was sweating from the hot soup or from his nerves.

She didn't answer right away. By the way her furrowed brows and pressed-together lips appeared now, she looked like she was struggling to give him an answer.

Then after what seemed to be a long time to Ross, she moved her head slightly back and forth in the international sign for a negative response.

"I am sorry but no. It is not that I would not like to, it is just that I cannot.

It is very complicated."

She looked as if she was pleading for him to understand. Even when she wasn't smiling she was beautiful. Her half-French, half-Vietnamese eyes looked right into his.

He asked, "Is there already someone special in your life?" Hoping that there wasn't.

"The only person in my life is my father."

He loved the sound of the way she pronounced **father**, with a French accent.

Genevieve wanted to explain the reason why she declined his invitation and found herself temporarily at a loss for words. Besides, this was neither the time nor the place. She had a tour to conduct and a schedule to keep. She took a pen and a piece of paper from her shoulder bag and wrote an address down. She slid the paper across the table to Ross.

She said, "Tomorrow evening at 6 o'clock, please come to that address. We can eat there and talk and I can explain myself better. OK?"

"Sure. OK. I'll see you tomorrow at 6 then," he replied with a smile.

He felt it was a small victory. Any chance to be with her was a small victory to him. He was a little bit surprised at this turn of events, a rejection promptly followed by an invitation. He didn't know if the address he'd been given was a restaurant, one of the sightseeing locations they'd been to or her own address. He was just glad he'd get to see her again. There was no denying it. He was attracted to her like a moth to a porch light in the middle of the night. He was just following his instincts.

Genevieve had turned the heads of some of the other men on the tour as well. Ross had noticed that right away. A few of the guys had commented about how attractive the young woman was, keeping their remarks clean for the most part.

    Ross showed up at the address Genevieve had given him, right on time. She was waiting for him at the front door of the building and looked very pretty in her black silk pants and gray pull-over short sleeve blouse.
    She asked him not to speak until they got up to the third floor of the stairwell. She didn't want her nosey neighbors to know that she was alone with him. She'd had company before, but always couples or other women she knew from school.
    Ross had ridden to the location in an open-air cyclo, this one powered by a motorcycle engine. The building was located down a narrow side street that connected directly into Trung Minh Ky, a wide boulevard that was quite long. He'd passed by the Army's 3rd Field Hospital on the way here. It was only about a quarter of a mile away.
    He was now in a building that had sturdy walls of cement, a solid three-story structure with similar buildings on either side of it. He'd noticed a couple of American civilians walking down the narrow street as he arrived, probably going home to apartments they rented. There were still lots of American civilians working and living in Saigon.
    Unlike the other apartments they'd passed while walking up the steps, Genevieve's apartment had an entrance on the outside of the building, at the end of a narrow balcony. All the others had doors in the central stairwell. He followed her in and then she locked the door. She took her security seriously.
    Her apartment was mostly just one very large room and a bathroom. It had a high ceiling with a ceiling fan slowly circulating

the warm humid air around some. There was a small table-top oscillating fan on a small wooden desk near the window facing the narrow street down below. There was a plain wooden chair at the desk, the type some people would use at their kitchen table. Genevieve had a queen size bed that was covered with a plain white sheet. Across the other side of the room from the foot of the bed stood an old dresser with six drawers and no mirror.

The walls of the apartment were a dingy white, badly in need of new paint. They were totally bare, no paintings, pictures or shelves.

On the side of the apartment furthest away from the front door, the only door there was, there was a tiled area. Some would call it a kitchenette. There was a sink and a small two-burner stove that was on a small wooden table near the sink. The table was bare oak, cracked in places by age. The stove was connected to a small six pound LP gas tank that was under the table and pushed up against the tiled wall. There was no refrigerator or other appliances.

Around the corner from the small kitchenette was an equally small tiled bathroom. It contained the bare essentials, a toilet, sink and shower. Ross noticed the absence of a shower curtain.

It was very evident to him that Genevieve was barely making ends meet as a tour guide. Either that or she had never intended to stay here for very long. Being observant of people and his surroundings was second nature to him now because it was a part of his job.

This was the first time that Ross had seen Genevieve in something other than an ao dai. The black silk pants and gray blouse made her look more petite somehow. She looked more attractive than ever. She had removed her sandals as soon as they were inside her apartment. He immediately noticed how small and pretty her feet were. Well-manicured, no polish. None on her fingers either. No trace of makeup on her face. Just a young beautiful woman who looked like she'd just gotten out of the shower and was in no need of anything to enhance her natural good looks. He couldn't take his eyes off her.

She offered him the only chair in the room and she sat on the bed.

"So, this is where you live?" he asked, realizing it was a dumb question afterwards.

"Yes, but it is only temporary," she replied, looking a little nervous.

Just then there was shouting from the street down below. Genevieve got up quickly and moved to the window, close to where Ross sat. She looked down at the people gathering together in a small crowd.

"Have you eaten yet?" she asked.

"No, not yet. Have you?"

"No. I was waiting for you so we could eat together. Excuse me while I buy food from the vendors. Just wait here."

She yelled something out the window, telling the vendors to wait for her. Then she grabbed a small purse from the dresser, slipped her sandals on and hurried out the door.

Ross peered out the window and watched as several people bought prepared food from two large food vendor carts. One had a charcoal grill on it and sold a variety of things that were cooked on bamboo skewers. He could see chicken, dried squid and fish. An iron pot held pho, the noodle soup he'd eaten for lunch the day before. It had tasted pretty good. The other vendor sold bread rolls and rice from his cart. Business was brisk to say the least. He continued to watch as Genevieve bought some food from both carts.

A short time later and she was back, placing their food on plates. They had room-temperature soda to drink since she didn't have a refrigerator, apologizing to Ross for that. He was happy when she provided a fork instead of a chopstick for him. He noticed that she was going to eat with a fork as well, possibly to make him feel more comfortable. They ate with their plates on their legs.

He waited until they finished eating the rice and chicken dinner before he began questioning her about what she'd said to him the day before. It had been on his mind since then.

"You said that it's not that you wouldn't like to have dinner with me but that you can't and it's complicated. Can you tell me exactly what you meant by that?"

Genevieve hesitated before answering, trying to think of the best way to explain her thoughts in English, which was not her native language.

She chose her words carefully, hoping he would understand.

"I do not know if you will understand. We have different cultures, different beliefs, different backgrounds and life experiences..." as her voice seemed to trail off.

Once again she hesitated, pausing to think.

Ross smiled at her, hoping to ease her discomfort and said, "Just pretend for a moment that I'm a long-time friend of yours and tell me whatever it is that's on your mind. Who knows, maybe I'll understand completely. Only one way to find out for sure, right?"

She seemed to relax a bit after he put her at ease. Her eyes widened slightly and she smiled back at him.

"Yes, OK. I will try to explain. My mother was Vietnamese and my father is French."

The way she pronounced the word **mother** sounded like **moth-air** to Ross, just like the word **father** sounded like **fath-air**, a French accent that he found sexy as hell. One more quality of hers that he found attractive. He hung on every word.

"My mother died in 1963. I was raised mostly in the Vietnamese culture but my education had a lot of French influence. Some people, including my father, say that many Vietnamese beliefs are based on superstitions and not real facts."

She paused and took a sip of her room-temperature soda. She could tell by the look in the handsome American's eyes and his facial expression that he was interested in what she was saying. He was leaning forward and looking directly at her.

Genevieve thought Ross had nice looking eyes. Were they hazel, gray or light blue? She couldn't tell for sure. They reminded her of her father's eyes whenever she spoke with him. Soft, kind, understanding. He was not making her nervous or uncomfortable at all by looking directly at her. Like he had said, like an old friend. In fact, she was now feeling at ease being alone with him.

She continued by saying, "Do you remember the day we met, when you slid under me to keep me from getting hurt when the guy pushed me down and stole my bag?"

"Just like it was yesterday," he replied.

"That was fate. It was meant to be. Just like my father from France, coming here to Vietnam and meeting by chance, by fate, my mother years ago. That was meant to be. So here I am, half-French, half-Vietnamese, talking to a man who came from America, the man that fate has brought into my life."

She sat there looking at him, smiling that beautiful smile of hers and paused, thinking of what to say next and how best to explain things so he would understand.

"I thought it would be unfair to you if I went out with you and you had no idea what you were getting involved in. Let me explain it this way. My father has an important position in a big shipping company owned by a very bad man. I have been warned by a man who is investigating the company my father works for. He told me that the bad man who owns the company has threatened to harm me and my father if my father does not do exactly what he is told. My father does not know that the investigator has talked to me."

Ross asked, "Do you know what agency the investigator works for?"

"The Vietnamese Central Intelligence Agency," she said, matter of factly.

"What exactly is he investigating? Did he tell you?" he asked, with obvious interest.

"He said my father's shipping company is suspected of helping the president of Vietnam become rich by selling large amounts of scrap metal that used to be American-made things like jeeps, trucks, things that the Vietnamese Army were given but could no longer be used. Also, large amounts of drugs. The owner of the company is very rich and very powerful. He has many corrupt political and military friends. My life and my father's life could be in danger if the owner is not satisfied with my father's cooperation."

Ross had been patiently sitting there and nodding his head every now and then as she spoke. With this new revelation, he was now more interested in her than ever before.

"So let me see if I've got this straight so far. Your father is being coerced by threats to you and him, from his boss, to help the shipping company help the president of Vietnam to get rich? And that's why it's complicated because if you're in danger, then anyone who is with you could be in danger too? Is that what you're saying?"

Genevieve smiled and nodded her head up and down in the affirmative.

"Yes. My father is an honest man. He would never do anything illegal. Because I am his only child and he loves me very much, he wants to keep me safe by doing whatever his boss tells him. I found out about the threats to me and my father from the investigator. It is for that reason that I am only staying in this place until my lease is up. Then I will move to a place that would be harder to find. If men working for the owner of the shipping company tried to kidnap me or kill me to punish my father, what do you think would happen if you were with me? You could get hurt or killed as well."

Genevieve's tone had changed noticeably. Ross could detect concern in her voice and it showed in her face. She was really worried, even for his safety. To him, it meant that she cared about him at least to some degree.

"Genevieve, I think I understand now. You **wanted** to say yes to my dinner invitation but couldn't because you wanted to tell me about a complication in your life, which you just did. And now, fate has made me a part of your complicated life. We're together right now, so I could be in danger too, as we speak. Is that right?"

"Yes. I am glad you understand. And I would not blame you if you chose not to see me again," she concluded.

There was a long moment of silence as the couple, brought together in this war-torn country by fate, sat facing eachother, trying to sense eachother's reaction and thinking about how to handle the awkward situation.

Ross broke the silence first.

"Do you feel safe living here by yourself?"

"Yes and no. I have nice neighbors and this part of the city seems to be nice and quiet. However, if the people working for my father's boss come here to harm me, then no, I do not feel safe here by myself," she explained.

"Then why don't you move in with your father? Wouldn't you feel safer then?"

"You do not understand." Genevieve's voice rose an octave as she replied, a sense of irritation that Ross noticed. "Why make it easier for my father's boss to get to us both at the same time? If they do not know where I live, I am safer. Above all, my father wants me to be safe and in no danger and I do too."

Ross regretted having asked that question right after hearing her answer.

"But they could find your office or get you while you're giving a tour, right?"

"Yes, and that is why I am going to close my business when I move from here, all because of the recent warning from the man investigating my father's business."

Once again there was a long moment of silence as Ross thought things over. There was a lot to think about. He took another drink of his warm soda. Not cold or even cool but at least it was wet and his throat had become very dry.

"You believe it was fate the day I helped you when the thief pushed you down and stole your bag, right?"

"Yes. It **was** fate. It was our destiny to meet that day. You saved me from being badly injured and you got my bag back for me. Thank you again for that. What else could it have been but fate?" She had made her feelings known very emphatically.

"And you're serious about closing your business and moving from here so you'll be harder to find, right?"

He realized that he was beginning to sound like a cop grilling a suspect and hoped she wouldn't be offended.

"Yes, as I already told you. I **have** to. I am going to move from here for sure. I have already made plans."

Ross nodded in understanding. Then he offered a plan of his own.

"I can't tell you exactly what my job is but I'm allowed to carry a gun everywhere I go. I can protect you and help you and your father with this problem. I'd like to help you."

Even though his focus was supposed to be on U.S. service members and their involvement with drugs and black marketing activities, he thought that there might be a connection between the shipping company and the drugs being sold to GIs. It wouldn't hurt to check and see. He hadn't done anything newsworthy lately. Maybe her father could help him out, maybe make a deal with him arranging a quid pro quo. He was willing to take a risk. A chance to spend more time with Genevieve would definitely be an added bonus.

That bit of information about carrying a gun really caught her off guard. Ross could see the surprised look on her face when her eyebrows arched upward and her mouth opened slightly as if she was forming the word "oh."

She had a worried tone in her voice when she spoke again. "But you are just one man. The company owner has many, many men. You would be in much danger too."

Ross replied, "There are lots of men that I can call on for help. Even regular military forces if need be."

His statement, made with complete confidence, caused her to pause and think it over.

"Why would you risk your life by getting involved in mine?" she asked out of curiosity.
  Ross kept his answer simple. "Like you said yourself, fate brought us together."

CHAPTER 13

Henri's brain tumor was getting worse. It was now causing him more pain and it had caused him to feint in his office. When he woke up the next day in a hospital, his daughter Genevieve was at his bedside. She was sitting in a chair and holding his hand, smiling at him. Seeing him open his eyes after so many hours made her very happy and somewhat relieved.

He felt so blessed to wake up to such a wonderful sight. To him, she was the most beautiful young woman in the world. It brought him a great feeling of relief and much joy to see her here by his side. It warmed his heart that his daughter cared about him so much. He felt like he was a lucky man in that regard.

The doctors had already done several tests on him since his arrival the day before. They already knew from previous tests that he had an inoperable cancerous brain tumor. There wasn't much they could do other than monitor his vital signs and give him something for the pain. That was little solace for a man who knew that his days on earth were now numbered.

Because Genevieve was the only family member that Henri had in Vietnam, the doctor treating him had to inform her about his condition. Henri's doctor didn't like having to give patients or their families bad news but that came with the job. Every oncologist received training for that painful experience but it didn't make the job any easier, especially if they knew the patient well. He was thankful for the clergymen who came to the hospital often, to assist him and other doctors in easing the pain and grief of patients and their loved ones. He welcomed all the help he could get. He preferred to leave the healing of hearts and souls to others.

When Dr. Hahn, her father's doctor, told her that his condition would only get worse, she broke down and cried. Genevieve then waited in the doctor's office until her eyes and face were no longer red and puffy before she took up her position in the chair next to her father's bed. She wanted to look strong for him, to give him hope even when there was none.

The relationship she had with her father was as good as the relationship she'd had with her mother, one of unconditional love. It had taken a long time for her to recover from the death of her mother. She dreaded even thinking about losing her father but now she knew that she had to begin the process of mentally preparing herself for that eventuality. Only a miracle could save her father now and she silently prayed for one.

"Hello, my dear. How are you?" Henri asked.

"I am fine, Papa. Your doctor told me all about your condition. I am so sorry," she said, as a tear ran down her left cheek. She tried not to cry in front of him but couldn't

help it.
 He could feel her tremble as her hand now began to shake slightly as it held his. He squeezed her hand tightly and said, "C'est la vie, n'est ce pas? You have to take the bad with the good sometimes, mon cheri."
 Having his own private hospital room made it easier for both father and daughter to be at ease and say whatever they felt without worry of being overheard or of disturbing another patient who may be asleep. Henri was not hooked up to any type of monitors now nor did he have an IV bottle or stand nearby to hinder their movements should he decide to get up out of bed. For the first time in a long while, the hospital wasn't full of sick or wounded civilians. Every couple of hours someone would stop in and take his temperature and check his blood pressure and pulse. He was going to be discharged as soon as the 24-hour observation period was over, as long as he didn't experience any more problems.
 Genevieve wiped her eyes dry then said, "Yes, Papa, the bad with the good. The doctor told me that you can go home tomorrow. They have done all the tests they need to do. You should be strong enough to go home but not strong enough to return to work. In a few days maybe, after you have rested some."
 She smiled over at his tired face and struggled with her thoughts. Should she tell him now, in the hospital, or wait until he was back in his own home? This couldn't wait, she finally decided, because her father's future was so uncertain.
 "Papa, Saturday night I will visit you at home and bring a friend that I want you to meet. Would that be alright?"
 "Sure, of course." That's a surprise. She's never brought a friend over to my home before. "Who is this friend, one of your old

classmates from school?"

"No, Papa. Remember the incident I told you about..."

"The one where you were shoved down by the guy stealing your shoulder bag during one of your tours?"

"Yes, that one. Well, I want you to meet the man who saved me from hitting the ground. He is an American and he went on one of my tours recently."

"Ah, so you got to meet him again?" Henri asked.

"Yes, Papa. And since that tour we have had dinner together and we talked a lot and I would like for you to meet him." Then she added, "And he wants to meet you too."

"Oh, really? He must be a really nice guy if you want to introduce him to me. You know, when I was your age, we had to like a person a lot before we would even consider introducing a person to our parents. Do you have any feelings for this guy, and by the way, what's his name?" her concerned father asked.

"His name is Tom Ross. And yes, I have feelings for him. How could I not? He practically saved my life. He is nice, tall, good looking and his eyes remind me of yours in some ways," she said.

She wasn't going to tell her father **everything**. No daughter does that. Some things were meant to be kept private.

"Well, if his eyes remind you of me, then he must be a good man, ha, ha," he joked, making light of it. Her visit was making him feel better already.

She's almost twenty years old, he thought. It's about time she found a good man to be with. Maybe this guy will be the right one for her. God, I hope so. I don't want her to be alone in the world after I'm gone. Saturday night can't get here soon enough.

Mang Binh Hoa didn't learn about Henri's stay in the hospital and his medical condition until after his return from Singapore. He was worried about Henri, but not because he really cared about him. It was because the position that Henri held in his company would be hard to fill once Henri died. Henri was much more than just an obediant employee. Those were a dime a dozen. He was intelligent, resourceful and had made many good business decisions that had helped the shipping company grow and prosper.

So far Henri had done everything that was asked of him. But, would he continue to do so? His safety and that of his daughter had been threatened and so far that had ensured Henri's compliance with Hao's wishes. But now, with Henri's death almost guaranteed by the cancerous brain tumor, might that give Henri the will to resist, the temptation to reveal Hao's wrongdoings to the authorities before he died?

Hao had most of the Cholon and Saigon authorities on his payroll already. So who could Henri turn to if he should decide to tell someone about Hao's illegal enterprises? Hao always tried to think of the future, to stay one step ahead of his competition and any adversaries. The only possible authority Henri could turn to, as far as he knew, was someone working for the South Vietnamese Central Intelligence Agency. One of Hao's paid informers gave him a name, Bui Van Nha. He'd been seen snooping around the Saigon River docks and talking to people, including Henri Ferrand. Hao decided that he needed to keep Henri around for as long as possible.

One of the main hiring locations for Vietnamese employees of U.S. facilities was the

Civilian Personnel Office in Saigon. It was at 28 Tran Qui Cap Street. There were a couple of reasons why there weren't many people there today. The U.S. government was reducing the numbers of its military forces at a rapid pace and many Vietnamese employed as day laborers, mama-sans, barbers, cooks, etc. were no longer needed. Also, there was a powerful typhoon out in the South China Sea and torrential rains and heavy winds were pounding most of the country.

The 101st Airborne Division at Phu Bai had left their base camp recently and the 3rd Brigade, 1st Cavalry Division (Airmobile), along with the 196th Infantry Brigade were preparing to pack up and leave for the United States in the very near future. Those units had provided thousands of South Vietnamese civilians with jobs and helped the local economy near their bases prosper, especially the bars, nightclubs, restaurants and hotels. That was the positive side.

Nearby orphanages were populated with many babies and young children who were half black and half Vietnamese and half white and half Vietnamese, along with many Vietnamese kids who had lost their parents to the war. That was the negative side. Like Henri Ferrand had told his daughter, Genevieve, you have to take the bad with the good sometimes.

Bui Van Nha was meeting with an employee at the Saigon Civilian Personnel Office on this dark and rainy day. The man was a paid informant of his and had some information to pass along. He'd been very trustworthy so far and Nha had no reason to suspect this new bit of information wouldn't be credible. The former South Vietnamese Army captain used several paid informants to help him in his investigations. Reliable information was important to any investigator and not always easy to obtain. Since the guy said he had some new "dirt" on Mang Binh Hao, Nha was immediately interested.

Nha had brought an umbrella with him but his white cotton dress shirt and gray dress pants still got wet anyway. Strong gusty winds blew the heavy rain almost sideways sometimes. His feet and sandals were thoroughly soaked.

Using his normal cover, he asked the informer if there were any jobs available for a man with only one hand. He had lost his right hand in combat and it limited his career opportunities. The man told him no, but slid a piece of paper across the desk to him. He told Nha to check with the people at that address and they might have some work for him. Nha grabbed the paper with his left hand, thanked the man, then stuffed it in his pants pocket. The drop had been completed. No one else in the office would have suspected a thing.

The slip of paper contained a short message. It told him to meet the informer at 7 that evening at the address of an apartment in Cholon, not far from a Chinese market. Nha had been on the main road where the market was and remembered its location. However, he was unfamiliar with the surrounding neighborhoods and side streets. It was an area consisting mostly of two and three story tall apartment buildings and small family businesses. Some of those businesses, like tire repair shops, took up the ground floor and the family owners lived upstairs in the second floor apartment. Accordian-like metal gates that were pulled across the front of the business and locked with a padlock, protected the establishments from thieves. The weather was so bad now that most of the small shops were closed and locked up.

The tropical downpours and gusty winds from the typhoon swept the city streets and sidewalks clean, eliminating the odors often smelled on hot, humid days. There was less traffic on the roads and very few people venturing outside too. Finding a taxi that night was no problem thanks to the bad weather. Several empty taxis were parked on a few street corners within easy walking distance for Nha.

Low clouds and pounding rain made it difficult for the driver to find the address Nha had given him. They passed right by it at least twice before finding it. To make matters even worse, the thunder and lightning had increased, making the driver a nervous wreck. He hated driving in this kind of weather but did it anyway because he needed the money.

Nha was looking forward to receiving some more information that would help him bring Mang Binh Hao to justice. He'd been pursuing the case he was building against Hao for a long time now. Some solid evidence would really be helpful and he was feeling optomistic about tonight. His informer at the Civilian Personnel Office had never let him down. He had a couple thousand piasters with him to reward the informant for the valuable information he'd been promised.

Even with the umbrella over his head, Nha still got wet again while running from the little dark blue and light yellow taxi to the door of the address. He kicked the door a couple of times with the sandal on his left foot since his only hand held the umbrella. His informer opened the door and quickly stepped aside.

The first thing Nha noticed when he entered the small apartment was a middle-aged woman in an ao dai, standing in the center of the small twelve foot by twelve foot room, directly under a bare 60-watt lightbulb that hung from the ceiling. They greeted each-other as the informant introduced her as his wife. Nha's peripheral vision detected some movement to his left rear, just behind the informant's right shoulder, coming out from behind the door that was now closing.

As he was about to turn his head in that direction to see what it was, lightning struck somewhere close by and the resulting thunderclap drowned out the sound of the gunshot that ended his life. The man who had hidden himself behind the front door was one of Mang Binh Hao's many guns-for-hire, a Chinese tong member from one of several gangs that operated in Cholon. He never missed a target from such close range. His extended arm had aimed the .45 caliber pistol right behind Nha's left ear. The fired round went clear through his head, knocking Nha a couple of feet closer to the center of the room. He was dead before his limp body hit the cement floor like a large sack of rice.

Hao's man told the couple to "di di mau" and they ran out into the dark stormy night. He took one last look at the gruesome scene on the floor. No need to check for a pulse. Shots to the head with large caliber guns usually made a mess and this was no exception. There was lots of blood and brain matter spread halfway across the room. There was no doubt that CIA agent Bui Van Nha was dead.

That was what he would tell Mang Binh Hao. The assassin then searched Nha's pockets and took the roll of money that had been meant for his trusted informant. So much for trust.

When the assassin reported back to Hao, he was given the other half of his fee. The deal had been half up front, half after the deed was done. Another loose end had been taken care of. Hao didn't like having to worry about someone discovering his secrets and so anyone he considered to be a threat or "unfinished business" was taken care of, permanently. That's what made Hao so dangerous.

CHAPTER 14

Vung Tau is a city located about 80 miles east of Saigon, at the eastern end of Highway 51. The French name for that city on a peninsula is Cap St. Jacques. Before 1954 and the end of French Indochina, the French governor general had his summer residence there, called the White Villa. It offered a break from the stifling heat and high humidity of Saigon.

It's a very picturesque resort town, with some amazingly beautiful beaches on the shores of the South China Sea. The brightly painted and often photographed Vung Tau lighthouse is just one of the many attractions there. It was built about a mile from the ferry landing, which also attracts a lot of visitors. Many tourists visited this scenic place and it became an in-country R & R (Rest and Recreation) center for American military personnel in the 1960s.

Unknown to the Americans, it was also an R & R location for the Viet Cong. That was the main reason they never attacked the city or their enemy within it. The only other places on the east coast of South Vietnam that came close to the beauty of this place and also became American in-country R & R centers were Cam Ranh Bay and China Beach, further north up the coast by Da Nang. The fact that many GIs ate at restaurants and sunned themselves on the beach with members of the Viet Cong eating and sunning themselves while only a few feet away from them, was just one of the many bizarre things about the war in Vietnam.

It was a very captivating and peaceful place to visit in order to get away from the ugly war that was being fought just a few miles inland to the west. The climate also offered the GIs some relief from the blazing heat and high humidity found in the jungles and rice paddies many of them had recently fought in.

A favorite place for many visitors to dine and stay overnight in Vung Tau, was the Metro Hotel. Located on Tran Hung Dao Street, it was an old French colonial building. It had arched windows and a red terra cotta roof that gave it the look of a three-story Mediterranean villa. In addition to the regular rooms, it had fully-furnished apartments for longer stays.

The large French restaurant on the ground floor served both French and Vietnamese food. American GIs could even get a decent milk shake, burger and fries there, all at very reasonable prices, especially considering the elegant French decor and friendly wait staff that was first-class all the way. All of the employees spoke Vietnamese, English and French, so "bon appetit" was a common phrase used there.

Brigadier General Minh Vinh Giang of the South Vietnamese Army Joint General Staff was wearing civilian clothes today instead of a uniform. He looked like he was dressed for a round of golf. None of the other diners in the Metro Hotel restaurant were dressed that way but then, they weren't wealthy generals either. His two bodyguards sat at a neighboring table. They wore blue jeans, gray T-shirts and low-cut black tennis shoes.

General Giang liked to copy the clothing styles of American men he saw in the magazines he perused in some of the MACV HQ offices he'd visited. The meetings he attended there with his American counterparts gave him an opportunity to see how they dressed when off-duty, at least in the magazines. He liked their colorful argyle socks, penny loafers with tassels, pleated tan slacks and light green polo shirts, which is exactly what he was wearing now. He didn't care much for the less colorful attire worn by most of the other Vietnamese staff members when off-duty. Even though he disliked both the French and Americans for interfering in Vietnamese internal affairs, he did like some things about them, notably French cuisine and American clothing.

He was here today to meet with Nguyen Quoch Dinh. They were both in their late forties, both military men and they both shared a dislike for all foreigners who tried to control the fate of the Vietnamese people, either by political or military means. Dinh and Giang had known eachother for a few years and as the Americans down-sized their remaining forces in their Vietnamization Program, the two men now met more frequently.

Nguyen Quoch Dinh was a high-ranking Viet Cong member of the Provisional Revolutionary Government. Brigadier General Minh Vinh Giang was a Viet Cong sympathizer and had been furnishing Dinh with military information for awhile. He used his position within the Joint General Staff to learn about tactical and strategic military plans. Then, if he thought there was valuable intelligence information like re-deployments of allied troops that would benefit the VC, he'd meet with Dinh at some pre-arranged location. Today they were having lunch together in Vung Tau, a safe haven for both VC and traitors alike.

Dinh also showed up for today's meeting accompanied by two bodyguards. They had to leave their AK-47 assault rifles behind and were armed only with switch-blade knives. Only military police and the city police were allowed to carry weapons in Vung Tau. His group of three men were all dressed like him. They wore long-sleeved white shirts with the sleeves rolled up, black tight-fitting slacks and what American GIs called "Ho Chi Minh" sandals.

The two VC bodyguards took a seat at a table adjacent to the one where the two bodyguards dressed in blue jeans sat. All three Viet Cong looked slightly thinner than the South Vietnamese soldiers. Their diet of mostly rice, fish and vegetables and the long distances they walked on a regular basis, had a lot to do with that.

General Giang and his bodyguards had arrived at the restaurant only a minute before Dinh and his men. They hadn't ordered any food or drinks yet. Giang smiled up at Dinh as his friend approached the table, then pointed at the seat across from him.

"Chao ong, Thieu Tuong Giang," Dinh greeted in a respectful tone. It meant, "Good afternoon, Brigadier General Giang."

"Chao ong, Dinh," replied the general, also in a respectful tone.

Vietnamese is a very tonal language. In other words, the tone or level of your voice changes the meaning of a word. "Ma," for example, when spoken in a level or middle tone can mean "ghost" or "to rub." If the same word is pronounced with a heavy tone, it means "rice seedling." So in speaking Vietnamese, tone is all-important.

Both men always spoke in lowered voices, just above a whisper, to keep their conversations as private as one could in a public place. They never met in private, always out in public and always with their bodyguards nearby.

A waitress approached their table to take their meal order after the general signaled her with a hand gesture and said, "Lai day," meaning, "Come here."

He ordered pho, a traditional Vietnamese noodle soup, and bottles of Ba Muoi Ba (the number 33), a Vietnamese brand of beer, for the men at all three tables. He also asked her to bring a bottle of nuoc mam, a smelly sauce made from fermented fish, to each table. Americans like their ketchup, Japanese like their soy sauce and Vietnamese like their nuoc mam.

After telling her that would be all for now, he finished with, "Cam on ong, mihn oi" (thank you, sweetheart).

She was young and very attractive, catching everyone's eye in her figure-enhancing violet ao dai. The traditional Vietnamese clothing she wore consisted of a tight-fitting violet long sleeve silk top that was split from the bottom to her slender waist and worn over loose-fitting white silk pants.

The general was married, the father of two girls and two boys. He was also a faithful husband. Still, the pretty waitress raised his blood pressure. She reminded him of his wife when they were first married; beautiful, petite and with a firm young body that drove him crazy with lust. Only his deep love and respect for his wife kept him from doing more than just exercise his eyeballs, admiring the lovely young lady. In that regard, he was much more restrained than a lot of men in his position of power, who often wouldn't hesitate to stray.

Nguyen Quoch Dinh thanked General Giang for the meal that he and his men were being treated to today. Then he joked, "Mihn oi?" What would your wife think if she heard you say that, ha, ha? She most certainly is a 'so mot' (number one) waitress!"

Vietnamese used a scale of numbers to grade things as being good or bad, just like American men did, except their system was in reverse. For example, an American male might look at a beautiful female and say to a friend, "She's definitely a ten," meaning, on a scale of one to ten, with one being the worst and ten being the best, she was the best.

When Dinh made a comment about the waitress being "so mot" (number one), that meant that she was the best. In Vietnam, "so mudi," (number ten) was the worst. Many GIs heard, "You numbah ten GI!" at one time or another during their tours of duty in Vietnam. If a Vietnamese was really upset at a GI, they might even say, "You xau lam, GI!" That meant, "You numbah ten thousand, GI!" which was extremely bad.

"What news do you bring from Saigon, general?" asked Dinh, as he added a few drops of golden brown nuoc mam sauce to his steaming hot bowl of pho.

The general added a few drops to his pho as well, then stirred it around a little with his white, wide, ceramic soup spoon. Then he leaned in towards Dinh as he blew on a spoonful of pho, cooling it down some, and said, barely above a whisper, "The American 101st

Airborne Division at Phu Bai will be leaving Vietnam for good in March."

He knew that if he was ever caught giving that kind of intelligence information to the Viet Cong, he'd be facing a firing squad for sure. Some traitors had already been disposed of in that manner. Only a double agent would be able to find out about his duplicity he thought, and he doubted that would ever happen.

He felt certain that, based on what he knew of his own country's military capabilities, the shrinking presence of American military forces, and the build-up in strength of Viet Cong and North Vietnamese forces, that the communists would unite the two Vietnams in the not-too-far away future and end foreign intervention once and for all. Dinh and others in the PRG had convinced him that the end of the current South Vietnamese government was near, and it was in his best interest to be on the winning side.

They would then be the masters of their own fate and peace would return to a land that had known war for so long. First it was the French who ruled their country, then the Japanese, followed by the French again. Although the Americans didn't come to rule over them, they had caused the killing and destruction to go on much longer than it would have otherwise, in his opinion. It might have been a case of good intentions gone bad but that didn't matter. The end result was all that mattered.

"Is that all? I could have found that out just by reading their Stars And Stripes newspaper. Every time one of their large units leaves, they hold a big ceremony, invite some South Vietnamese generals or President Quoch, and print pictures with the story, for all to see," Dinh stated, rather sharply. His furrowed brows and frown added emphasis to his displeasure.

"Yes, but now you know, well in advance of any public release of that information. And, there is more," General Giang replied. "Do you know General Le Long Quang, the South Vietnamese commander of IV Corps in the Mekong Delta?"

"Not personally, why?"

"I heard that he's under investigation for selling rice to Viet Cong forces in his area of responsibility. There have been rumors that he and the VC commander he has been dealing with, might be on a Phung Hoang (Phoenix Program) list to be 'neutralized' instead of being arrested," he stated, matter of factly.

General Giang then took a drink of his Ba Muoi Ba and pushed away his empty soup bowl. The pho had satisfied his hunger. He looked across the table at Dinh, wondering what kind of reply he would get from the stoic-looking Viet Cong leader. He then looked around quickly and noticed that all four bodyguards were finished eating as well. They looked tired and bored as they silently sipped their beer. None of them had spoken a word since they had arrived as far as he was aware. Then he looked back at Dinh again.

"I'll get word to the commander of our forces in the Delta about what you just told me. I'll be on that list too if the Americans find out that I own the building on Cong Ly Boulevard in Saigon that they lease for one of their billets. All of that money they spend is used to finance our organization, paying for weapons, medical supplies, food and for paying off high-ranking government and military officials."

General Giang's eyes widened a little and the expression on his face changed from deadpan to one of surprise upon hearing that news. He was unaware that Dinh was collecting rent on his property from the U.S. government.

Dinh took a long swallow and finished his beer. Then he added, "But of course they would have to catch me, which we both know will never happen."

Then he laughed a little as he smiled and the general laughed politely too, knowing it was all true. He didn't collect the rent in person. He used a middle-man to act as property owner and to get the money.

"Isn't it ironic that the U.S. government is unknowingly providing financial support to the very forces that it is fighting against, simply by paying rent on a building in Saigon to house some of its troops?" Dinh asked. An evil-looking smirk was evident on his face as he spoke.

"I'll tell you something else that is ironic," stated Giang, wanting to impress Dinh with his own guile. "They even paid for our meal today too!" he stated with a big grin.

"How so?"

"One of their generals gave me a bottle of expensive bourbon as a gift last week. I sold it on the black market for ten thousand piasters! At the current exchange rate of 250 piasters for one American dollar, that's double what that dinkai dau (crazy) general paid for it, ha, ha!"

They both laughed at that as they rose from their seats, signifying the end of their meeting.

"As always, General Giang, your information is much appreciated. May it help bring about our victory that much quicker."

To that, Giang added, "The sooner the better, Dinh. The sooner the better."

CHAPTER 15

Linda's Surprise Bar was almost filled to capacity and already very noisy by the time Navy Lieutenants Daniel Ventnor and Bob Kosinski arrived. It was now early in the evening, just after sundown on the outskirts of Saigon. The two men were in their civvies, just like the rest of the American GI patrons of the popular hangout. They were on duty with the mission of discovering if any GIs there were buying or selling drugs, particularly interested in any Navy SEAL team members about to leave the country. Some teams that had already gone back to the States had smuggled large amounts of drugs out of Vietnam and now these two members of the 1st Speial Investigations Unit were following up on some leads. They knew that all SEAL teams remaining in Vietnam were scheduled to leave the country this year so it was a time-sensitive issue.

Both investigators ended up sharing a table with two other off-duty GIs who, coincidently, turned out to be members of SEAL Team 1. They were scheduled to leave the country in a couple of days and wanted to enjoy one last floor show at Linda's. Cigarette, cigar and pipe tobacco smoke clouded the acrid air, giving it a thick blue haze throughout the tawdry joint. A few hand-rolled joints added to the smoky atmosphere.

Shortly after Bob and Daniel were served their drinks by a cute waitress, the floor show started. Loud whistles and vulgar catcalls greeted the naked Vietnamese man and woman as they stepped out from behind a curtain that bordered the back of a small stage. An overhead spotlight was shining down on a mattress covered by a white fitted sheet. On most nights, this was where live bands were set up. On either side of the stage were go-go dancer cages mounted on small sturdy platforms. The cages were painted with a special paint so whenever they were occupied with go-go dancers, black lights were turned on them and they would glow in the dark for that discotheque look.

The audience didn't know the naked couple was married, nor would they have cared. All they cared about was watching a live sex show with a very slender and pretty 20-something female and her well-endowed male partner, also in his twenties.

The young Vietnamese couple wasted no time on foreplay. They got into the 69-position first and engaged in oral sex for a while. After a few minutes of that they proceeded to get it on like two dogs in heat, changing positions every two minutes or so it seemed, to the total delight of the cheering crowd.

The live sex act lasted for about twenty minutes and ended with loud moans and groans from the couple, signaling dual orgasms, probably faked in order to please the crowd of onlookers who wouldn't have known one way or the other. Then they stood up on the mattress and joined hands and took a bow as if they were actors on a stage at the conclusion of a Broadway play. The patrons of Linda's then stood up and gave them a standing ovation, with more loud whistles and vulgar catcalls. Half of the crowd had been standing already, trying to get a better view of the lurid sex acts being performed on the stage.

After the naked couple disappeared behind the curtains and the noise died down some, Daniel and Bob were able to talk with the other guys at their table. They had decided to use a cover story prior to entering Linda's and would say that they worked in the MACV Public Affairs Office. That would make sense to anyone wondering why they asked so many questions. Public Affairs people were like other types of journalists, always looking for a story.

The two off-duty GIs introduced themselves as Pete and Anders. They both came from aviation backgrounds. Pete was an Aviation Ordnanceman and Anders was an Aviation Electrician's Mate First Class. They were both members of SEAL Team 1, based at My Tho, about 60 miles from Saigon, on the My Tho River. Bob and Daniel took turns buying Pete and Anders rounds of beer, hoping to loosen up their tongues. They told them how much they admired the men in the SEAL teams. They sipped on their own beer very slowly. After all, they were on the job.

Their plan only partially worked. They were able to learn that part of SEAL Team 1 would be flying from Bien Hoa aboard a Navy C-47 that would take them to Cubi Point Naval Air Station in the Philippines.

Bob asked the two SEALS, "Where's your home base?"

Anders answered, "We're flying into Naval

Air Station North Island in Coronado, California. We're stationed on the west coast." His tongue was getting thick and his speech was slightly slurred but Bob managed to understand him, barely.

Then Daniel asked, "Is the whole team going on the same plane?"

Ander's partner, Pete, looked at Daniel in a suspicious way. Then he said, "No, some of the guys are flying out of Tan Son Nhut on a Navy C-119. Why you wanna know?" He was having some difficulty talking without slurring his words too.

Then he asked, "Say, where you guys work anyway? Why so many questions?" A loud belch followed his last word. Even the belch was slurred.

Daniel answered, "Public Affairs, over at MACV. We're the guys that put stories about you guys in your hometown newspapers. That is why we ask everyone for their names and home towns and stuff."

Bob shook his head up and down in agreement, hoping their cover story would satisfy them. He and Daniel kept smiling, trying to remain cool and friendly. The last thing they wanted was trouble. Especially from Navy SEALS. They were just average in size while Pete and Anders were not.

Pete was six one and built like a fire hydrant, looking as solid as a bronze statue. Anders was even taller and larger in every respect. The Swede was six five, two hundred twenty five pounds and had muscles on his muscles. His neck was so thick, he almost looked like he didn't have one. His hands were huge. When he held his beer mug, it looked like a miniature one instead of a normal one. The only way an opponent would stand a chance of not being pummeled to death in a fight with him would be to kick him in the nuts and then run like hell.

A waitress came up to their table and asked the four men if they were ready to order some more beer. She wore the standard waitress outfit of Linda's, a white T-shirt with the bar's name printed on the front and back in big red letters and a bright red mini-skirt that showed off her shapely legs. As she was leaning across the table and wiping it off with a rag, giving Bob, Daniel, Pete and Anders a big smile, a hand went up her skirt and groped her right ass cheek.

A customer from a nearby table had seen the lower part of her round buttocks as her mini-skirt rose up her behind when she bent over. Her white cotton panties were in stark contrast to the bright red of her mini-skirt and her tan skin. She quickly turned around and slapped the guy's hand away, saying loudly and angrily, "Choi oi! Do ma nhieu!"

The guy who was just trying to "cop a feel" as he called it, jerked his stinging hand back in reaction. He just smiled at her and said, "You number one girl."

With anger in her voice, she replied, "You numbah ten GI! Do ma nhieu!" and walked away in a hurry. She went straight to the bar to tell her manager. She was a new girl and was not used to being groped.

The half-drunk GI just laughed it off and asked one of his buddies, "What did she say?" Nobody at his table had a clue.

Pete, a little upset that a guy from another table would mess with his waitress while she was taking drink orders at his, leaned over towards the guy so he could be heard above the din caused by jukebox music and loud voices.

"Hey buddy, what did you do to get my waitress so pissed off?"

"I just felt her up a little, no big deal.

What did she say anyway? I don't speak Vietnamese. Do you?"

Pete told him, "She told you to go fuck yourself."

The guy's eyes went wide and he stood up. "Well, we'll just see about that, that little bitch!"

Before he could take a second step towards the bar, Pete grabbed the back of his shirt just below his neck and jerked him back into his seat. Seeing that, the three other guys at the jerk's table got up and came to his defense. It was on now!

Anders stood up so quick to jump into the free-for-all that he accidently knocked the table over onto Bob and Daniel, sending them in their chairs over backwards into the customers sitting behind them. Before they knew it, the two investigators were soaked in beer, bruised from the fall to the floor and were now being set upon by total strangers who began kicking and punching them while they were still on the floor.

The inside of Linda's Surprise Bar soon took on the look of a scene from a Hollywood movie, an old Western saloon fight with cowboys throwing people out of the big front window, chairs crashing down on heads, and bodies landing on the sidewalk just beyond the front door.

It didn't take long before the Vietnamese military police, the Quan Canh, and the National Police, the Canh Sat, to show up. The Canh Sat were easily recognizable by their white gloves and white helmets. GIs called them "white mice." So far no American MPs had shown up. In the ensuing confusion caused by the language barrier and in identifying who was guilty and who was innocent in the chaotic bar fight, Bob and Daniel managed to get back to their billet that night with only a few minor cuts and bruises. They had not been taken in by any of the police forces that showed up nor had their cover been blown. More importantly, they'd gotten some information which may prove to be valuable in their investigation. In addition, they'd gotten to see a live sex show and enjoy some cold beer while on duty. Not a bad night, all things considered.

Late in the afternoon of the following day, Lieutenants Ventnor and Kosinski reported the previous night's findings to their CO, Captain Greg Daniels. They gave him all the details of the fight and floor show too, which helped explain their roughed-up appearance. Captain Daniels then got in touch with Navy authorities at Cubi Point Naval Air Station, near the big Navy base at Subic Bay, Philippines. They would have the two planes carrying SEAL Team 1 searched as soon as they landed.

Since two different types of planes were leaving from two separate bases in Vietnam, the drug sniffing dogs and their handlers would have twice the amount of hot, tedious work to do. Whenever aircraft sat on the hot, humid flightline after their engines shut off, the interiors became like ovens very quickly. It was hard working conditions for both dog and man alike.

Larry Hanks left his residence at 190 Pasteur Street each morning at a different time and by a different route to get to work each day. He was the assistant security man at the Civilian Personnel Office in Saigon and his own personal security was very important to him. It was only a short distance from his residence on Pasteur Street to his office on Tran Qui Cap.

For the second time in six months, an employee of the Civilian Personnel Office had been executed by the Viet Cong. That put him and everyone who worked there on edge. That was why he varied his times and routes of travel. Whenever the VC executed someone, they often did it in a way that sent a message to others and to put fear in those who would oppose them. In both matters, they usually succeeded.

The latest victim was found not far from his own residence in Cholon. The South Vietnamese police had not located his wife yet in order to tell her. The man's throat had been cut and his tongue cut out. That kind of message usually meant the victim had talked to the wrong people.

Only the day before, the body of Bui Van Nha had been found, also in Cholon. The police weren't sure if these two murders were connected in any way. Just the same, from what his friends had told him, Larry Hanks was taking no chances. If the VC killed one of his employees, they may find a reason to come after him, especially if they found out that a couple of his friends were involved in the Phoenix Program, created to round up or "neutralize" the leaders and cadres of Viet Cong.

Nguyen Quoch Dinh and Mang Binh Hao were both satisfied now that two loose ends had been taken care of. With the death of Nha and his informant, they had no plans to bother with Hanks. Dinh, the high ranking VC member of the Provisional Revolutionary Government, was only too happy to assist his friend Hao with the death of Nha's informant. Hao could have taken care of it himself but decided to make it look like a genuine VC "hit" by having them actually do it their way. A shot to the head might have caused the authorities to connect the two deaths but this way they had to follow two trails instead of one.

"A very well thought-out plan, Hao," Dinh complimented his wealthy supporter.

"It pays to be clever, my friend," Hao replied. He raised his cup of tea for a toast. "To our northern brothers and their success."

"Yes, to their success," Dinh agreed, then raised his cup and clinked it against Hao's. "Tomorrow can't get here soon enough."

As their private meeting ended in the small Chinese restaurant in Cholon, North Vietnamese armies prepared to strike in three different parts of the country. The Viet Cong were still not as strong in manpower as they had been in 1968 at the beginning of the Tet Offensive. That was one reason why they would leave the heavy fighting in the upcoming offensive to the NVA. Meanwhile, Dinh would continue training and recruiting for his build-up of forces and Hao would continue undermining the South Vietnamese and American's fighting effectiveness by whatever means he could. The fewer troops they could put in the field against the NVA, the better. There was a steady increase in the numbers of soldiers put out of action by drug use. That was one of Hao's contributions to the war effort.

On March 30, 1972, North Vietnamese Army forces launched their offensive against South Vietnam. They called it the Nguyen Hue campaign. Americans called it The Easter Offensive. At the time there were only about 69,000 U.S. soldiers left in South Vietnam. Around 5,000 of those were assigned as military advisors to South Vietnamese army units. Many others were responsible only for local security duties near their base areas and many more were support personnel on the main bases and not out

in the field.
   Unlike previous offensives, this one included large numbers of tanks and heavy artillery in each of the three areas of the country attacked. Those American bases not directly attacked by NVA tanks and infantry were targeted and hit with 122mm Russian-made rockets, some fired by Viet Cong forces, others by NVA units.
   On April 7, 1972, four rockets hit Bien Hoa Air Base, about 17 miles northeast of Saigon. A week later Tan Son Nhut Air Base, on the northwest side of Saigon was hit by a rocket. The air base also served as an international airport, so the effects of a single rocket hitting anywhere near civilian airliners full of passengers was big news on a major scale. Another rocket aimed at the base had missed and hit a marketplace nearby. It killed twelve innocent men, women and children and wounded four others.
   Two weeks later, three more rockets hit Bien Hoa Air Base, also a busy airport with many civilian airliners transporting American GIs to and from Vietnam. While those rocket attacks were nothing compared to the pounding artillery and tank assaults against Quang Tri, Kontum and An Loc, they took lives and destroyed buildings and military equipment just the same.
   For many U.S. troops that entered the war through the major air bases in South Vietnam, their first day "in-country" would be their last. 997 soldiers were killed on their first day in Vietnam. After having already completed their tours of duty, 1,448 soldiers were killed on their last day in Vietnam. In this war with no front lines, any day for any American in Vietnam could be their last. It was just that kind of war.

CHAPTER 16

It had been awhile since Captain Daniels contacted his Navy counterparts in the Philippines. He wondered if they had found anything on either of the two planes he had called them about. He sat at his desk and sipped his first cup of coffee of the day, trying to get fully awake. He found that reading over routine military paperwork was like reading a boring book, it almost put him to sleep. Now he had a caffeine habit, drinking up to six cups of coffee to get through each day.

As his IN box slowly emptied, he found a brown envelope addressed to him. In it was a copy of a Navy report that he found to be anything but routine and definitely not boring. Finally, something about the Navy SEALS. He read it and was happy that his unit's tip and their part of the investigation led to some positive results. He'd soon be sharing this news with his boss and everyone else in the 1st Special Investigations Unit. This was the kind of paperwork he actually enjoyed reading with his morning coffee.

In summary, the report named four members

of Navy SEAL Team 1 who were caught smuggling heroin out of Vietnam and into the Philippines. The four men had prepared the required military documents for their personal possessions and SEAL team equipment for Customs inspections. They loaded everything, including the heroin, which they hid in some of their personal belongings, inside of a CONEX box, the standard metal military shipping container they always used.

The men had traveled this route before, from Tan Son Nhut Air Base in Saigon to Cubi Point Naval Air Station near Olongapo City, Philippines. They had never encountered any problems with customs inspections or anything before. What they didn't know was, a new aircraft inspection procedure had recently been put in place and it caught them totally off guard. Drug sniffing dogs were now being used to thoroughly check all aircraft arriving in the Philippines from Vietnam and Thailand. That was something Philippine President Ferdinand Marcos insisted upon since some of the drugs in his country originated in Thailand and South Vietnam, according to his advisors.

One of the dogs alerted on the CONEX shipping container on the old C-119 transport plane. Cargo handlers were then called in to remove it from the plane with a forklift. It was opened right there on the flightline and searched. The specially trained dog had no problem discovering the hidden drugs. Since the seabags and wooden seachests had the owner's names stenciled on them, authorities had an easy job identifying the four SEAL team members.

Instead of returning to their home base in California like their team members who flew in the C-47 out of Bien Hoa did, these four men ended up in Fort Leavenworth, Kansas, where military members convicted of serious crimes are incarcerated. Captain Daniels finished reading the report just as he finished his third cup of coffee. The day was far from over and it had gotten off to a pretty good start.

    Henri Ferrand was feeling very tired even though it was still early in the evening when his daughter and her guest showed up. The powerful pain medication he was taking sometimes made him feel tired and drowsy. He was sitting in his favorite soft, over-stuffed, black leather armchair with his feet propped up on a cushioned footstool in matching black leather.
    The light hanging from the ceiling in his livingroom cast a soft glow on everything. Like many houses in Saigon, he used 60-watt lightbulbs to help conserve electricity. Brown-outs and black-outs happened at least once or twice a week because of the strain put on the old electrical system of the city. The Vietnamese government had done very little in the way of modernization since the French had left in the early 1950s. The French had left them with a fairly modern city some referred to as "The Paris of the Orient" because of so much architecture and wide tree-lined boulevards that mimicked Paris. Now it was in bad need of repair and modernization.
    Henri felt pride in what he and his fellow countrymen had done for this former colony, once a part of Asia that was called French Indochina. He was especially proud of what he had done himself in making his shipping company one of the largest and prosperous, not only in this country but in all of Southeast Asia. The Gulf of Lion Shipping Company was much larger now than when he first started

working for it in Vung Tau so many years ago.

    The recent death of Bui Van Nha had shocked and saddened Henri and caused him much stress. The murder had been mentioned in all the newspapers, on TV and in radio broadcasts as well. He had considered turning over his journals to Nha in hopes of seeing justice done. Now he worried that he'd die before finding someone to give them to, someone he could trust and was in a position of authority.

    The housemaid answered the knock at the door when Genevieve and her guest arrived. After a quick greeting, she led them into the livingroom. Then she excused herself and went into the adjoining kitchen to prepare tea for the guests she'd been told to expect.

    "Bon soir, Papa," Genevieve greeted her father. "How are you feeling?"

    "Bon soir, mon cheri. A little tired, that's all. Nothing to worry about," he lied. He was more than just a little tired. He was slowly dying.

    "Papa, this is Lieutenant Tom Ross, the man I told you about. Tom, this is my father, Henri Ferrand."

    Henri stood up slowly and reached out to shake his hand. He was pleased as he felt a handshake that was strong but not too strong. Henri didn't like men who tried to impress you with their youthful strength by squeezing your hand real hard. This young man had a friendly smile and his handshake had genuine warmth in it. And his eyes, yes, he could see what his daughter meant when she had mentioned his eyes before. He returned the smile.

    "It's a pleasure to meet you sir," Ross said. He could see how tired Henri looked, even though the older man did his best to try and hide it behind a smile.

    "The pleasure is all mine, I assure you.

And please, call me Henri. Formalities are good in some circumstances but I am at home now and you are a welcome guest in my home, so please, call me Henri."

"Yes sir. Henri it is. Thank you."

Before they could begin any conversation, the housemaid entered the room with a tray and held it out for each of them to take a cup of hot tea. She was a middle-aged woman and wore the traditional ao di of black silk pants and long white tunic. She'd been working for Henri since he and his wife and daughter moved to Saigon a long time ago. He trusted her to not repeat to others anything said in his house. Mai was like a part of his family.

Ross took a small sip, careful not to burn his lips and embarrass himself. He took a quick look around the room. It was about the size of his parent's livingroom in Oklahoma. He'd never been to France and wasn't sure how the people there decorated their homes. He was pretty sure that no American had a hand in decorating this one.

Each window had long curtains that almost reached the floor. Their dark blue color went well with the light blue walls. There were many oil paintings throughout the house, each one in a fancy gold-tinted frame. The floor lamp and table lamp looked like they were of an ornate design that may have been popular in Europe at the beginning of the twentieth century. Even the heavy-looking metal table fan looked antique. The chair that Henri sat in and the couch he and Genevieve sat on looked outdated but only slightly worn. The smell of leather reminded him of his old Little League baseball glove.

Ross sipped his tea and politely waited for Genevieve to take the lead. He felt a little nervous because he wasn't sure how things would go. But, he **had** volunteered to help them and that was why he was here.

Genevieve began speaking to her father in French and paused shortly afterwards to apologize to Ross, telling him of her need to explain some things to her father in his native language. Ross understood completely and told her so. He just sat there and listened, amazed at not only how fast she spoke but how beautiful the French language sounded, especially when spoken in Genevieve's soft feminine voice. He was captivated by their conversation. He didn't speak the language so he had no clue that a lot of their discussion was about him.

"Papa, I know you do not agree with or believe in many Vietnamese beliefs but at least please listen and try to understand me. Fate has brought this man and I together, just like fate brought you and Mother together."

Before she could explain anything further, Henri interrupted her. "If that is true, and I accept that it might be, then you didn't bring him here just because he told you that he wanted to meet me. There is more to this visit, right?"

She couldn't deny it. "Yes, I feel that I love him, Papa. I have not told him yet. You told me before, after Mother died, that I may choose my marriage partner and do not have to follow the Vietnamese tradition in that regard. N'est ce pas?"

"Oui, d'accord. How does he feel about you? Do you have any idea?" the concerned father asked.

She responded, "I know that he cares enough about me to offer his help and protection. And he asked to meet you to extend his offer of help to you as well. He would not do such a thing if he did not care about me."

Her statement surprised him and it was evident in the tone of his voice when he asked, "Help and protection? Help and protection from what? What are you talking about?"

The change in the sound of her father's voice made Genevieve nervous about telling him what she knew. She had always told him the truth and wasn't about to lie or mislead him so she just came straight out with it.

"One day a man told me that Mang Binh Hao had blackmailed you with threats to your life and mine if you did not do exactly as you were told. He said that he works for the Vietnamese Central Intelligence Agency and that he has been investigating Hao's shipping company for some time. He told me he thinks the scrap metal sales and drug smuggling are the connections between Hao and government officials and maybe even the Viet Cong. The man said it was only fair for me to know of the threats made by Hao so I can be on guard and protect myself somehow. Then he told me that you would not know that I would be informed. He thought that you would not tell me because you did not want me to become frightened. The same reason you did not tell me about your cancerous brain tumor. N'est ce pas?"

That got Henri's attention, unaware that she knew.

"How do you know about that?"

"A little bird told me."

"A little bird, huh?" He was thinking of his oncologist, one of only a few who knew about it. Until now.

"Saigon is full of little birds. They are everywhere," Genevieve stated matter-of-factly.

Still surprised at her discovery, Henri turned to Ross.

"Would you care for some more tea? I'm sorry that you have been left out of the conversation but it seems that my daughter has brought more to discuss with me than just the weather. Please excuse us."

"I'm fine, thank you. I'm afraid I'm not much of a tea drinker. It's OK," Ross said, "Fathers and daughters need to talk about things. I completely understand."

Actually, he didn't. He just didn't know what else to say and was just being polite. He only hoped the evening ended well for everyone concerned. Based on their voices and tone, it sounded like a pretty serious discussion, especially when paired with their facial expressions as they spoke. You didn't have to speak the language to sense that a serious topic was being discussed. He was intuitive enough to realize that.

Turning back to Genevieve, Henri told her, "Oui, mon cheri. That is why I did not tell you. And did you know, the man who told you those things about Hao was found murdered recently?"

"No. He did not tell me his name. You mean to say, the story on the evening news and in the newspapers was about the same man? Are you sure?" she asked in a high-pitched voice. Fear and surprise were reflected on her face.

Ross didn't understand what they were saying but he noticed the look on Genevieve's face. "What's wrong, Genevieve?"

She turned to look at Ross as Henri answered her, "Yes, I'm sure."

She told Ross about the man who had warned her and who had been investigating her father's company.

"Murdered? Holy cow!" he exclaimed. "Tell your father about my offer to help keep you safe and to help him too. Go ahead, tell him now," he insisted.

Henri understood him and spoke English better than his daughter realized. He was curious as to what Ross had in mind.

Genevieve then reached out a hand and leaned forward and touched her father's knee. She began speaking softly and quickly, again in his native tongue.

"Papa, Tom is authorized to carry a gun with him wherever he goes as part of his job. He has others who can help also, to help you and I stay safe. He told me that he wants to meet you and offer his help. That is why I have brought him here with me."

Replying in French, Henri told her, "That means he is either regular military police or an investigator of some kind. As with the man who was murdered recently, that can be both a blessing and a curse." Henri paused to sip some tea before it got cold. He needed some time to think things through.

He turned slightly to look at Ross and said in halting English with a French accent, "Thank you for what you did before to help my daughter and for offering to help us now. Merci beau coup."

"You're welcome."

Ross glanced out of the corner of his eye at Genevieve and saw that she was looking directly at him and smiling. Henri noticed it too, also noticing that she had moved right up to Ross, her right arm now pressing against his left. Well, she was old enough to be on her own and decide for herself what she wanted to do with her life. He wouldn't interfere. It was clear to Henri that his daughter wanted to be with this American. Only time would tell how that would work out.

Henri then asked Ross, "What can you tell me about your job and how you might be able to help us?"

"I'm an Air Force investigator. It's a fact that many American GIs use drugs and some are involved in drug smuggling. It's my job to help solve the problem. Genevieve told me about the man who was investigating your company and about his warning to her. There might be a connection between your company and the drugs ending up in the hands of GIs. I'm just one of many who are investigating the drug problem around Saigon and the nearby American bases. That's why I can always get more help if I need it, and that includes personal protection for you and Genevieve." Ross hesitated a moment and then added, "Please don't mention to anyone what I just told you. It's very important that nobody knows what my job is. I'm only telling you all this because I know your daughter is living in fear and she fears for your safety as well. I really think that I can help keep you both safe."

Henri just nodded his head but didn't reply while he let that information sink in for a moment. He began thinking of some possible scenarios that might affect the futures of both he and his daughter if he took Ross up on his offer of help.

One scenario had a definite outcome. His cancerous brain tumor would surely leave him dead and Genevieve would be left alone to fend for herself. He couldn't do anything about the brain tumor but he hit upon an idea to do something about his daughter's situation. He would match the offer of help with one of his own.

The first meeting between Henri and Ross had ended with Henri telling them that he would think about the offer but that, because he was feeling very tired, he needed to sleep on it. Then they could come back for another visit and discuss the details.

Genevieve felt relieved about their visit and the introduction of Ross to her father. In her opinion, things had gone well.

Ross left Henri's house that evening feeling optimistic too but felt bad that Genevieve's father had a cancerous brain tumor. He felt bad for both of them. He had seen, even felt to a degree, the love between father and daughter. Now he had to figure out a way to help them.

CHAPTER 17

In the pre-dawn hours of May 17, 1972 and only 18 miles northeast of Genevieve's apartment in Saigon, the lights went out in a flash, literally, for Private First Class David Hart. He was knocked unconscious, but only momentarily. The funny thing was, he didn't feel a thing. When his thought processes began to work again, he wasn't sure if he was dead or alive.

Why can't I see anything? Why can't I hear anything? Why can't I feel anything? Am I alive? Was that bright flash I'd seen, the white tunnel I'd heard about, the brightly-lit path leading to Heaven? Why can't I move? He was starting to get scared and he didn't scare easily.

His favorite song on Armed Forces Network radio started playing in his head. Then, for some unknown reason, an unrecognizable voice told him to forget about it, get over it, the past was the past and he had to move on. The music brought back painful memories of a lost love, but he loved that music and the lyrics so much, even though it sometimes brought him to tears, like now.

He thought his eyes were tearing up. He had no way of knowing that it was blood running from his eyes and not tears. No song on earth could do that to a young man, but the concussive effects of an exploding 122mm Russian-made rocket could.

PFC Hart suddenly thought of his moma. He sure did miss her now. He wanted to call out to her but couldn't. He made a mental effort to, but didn't make a sound. He had no idea that his entire lower jaw was missing. The only thing that kept him from drowning in his own blood was the way his body was positioned when it hit the ground. His head was tilted slightly downward, kept above the ground an inch or two by a piece of debris that was once a part of the Post Exchange that was now in ruins all around him. His helmet and M-16 lay on the ground nearby, both partially covered with rubble from the PX.

The bright white light that PFC Hart had thought about was caused by the detonation of a six-foot, one hundred pound rocket. It had been fired from within four miles of his 1st Cav unit at Bien Hoa. The noise from the explosion was like a clap of thunder, so loud that he could feel it in his bones, as well as hear it. Upon impact, thousands of shards of metal, some as small as a dime, others two feet long, sliced through the air so fast they couldn't be seen.

He didn't hear the tremendous explosion of the ammo storage facility at the edge of his unit's perimeter when it took a direct hit from another rocket. Flames from that inferno shot up hundreds of feet into the night sky. It could be seen a mile away by airmen at the air base on the opposite side of the runway from the 1st Cav positions. The blast of the rocket that hit near him had blown out his eardrums.

The twenty-year-old soldier, now a PFC in the Army and four months into his twelve-month tour, was fading in and out of consciousness. He'd been near the entrance of the PX when the attack began. He'd been a regular customer there, buying razor blades, soap, snacks, normal stuff that GIs in camp needed.

The explosion that destroyed the PX, sent him flying through the air at first, as if he weighed next to nothing. Then he hit the ground as gracefully as a sack of potatoes. He was returning to his hootch after his stint of guard duty was over. His helmet and flack jacket had, no doubt, kept him from being even more seriously injured. As it was, he was bleeding from his eyes, ears and the lower half of his face where his lower jaw used to be.

The 1st Cavalry Division units at Bien Hoa, located only a short distance northeast of the air base runway, had been relatively lucky in a way. There were helicopter and artillery units there, plus fuel and ammunition storage areas. There was a dispensary and a drug treatment/rehabilitation center with dozens of patients. There were also rows upon rows of hootches that were full of sleeping troops when the attack began.

As bad as the damage was, it could have been much worse. Not a single helicopter or artillery piece was put out of commission. The fuel storage bladders hadn't been hit and the two buildings that were destroyed, a helicopter repair hanger and the Post Exchange, could easily be rebuilt with the help of the Navy Seabees from the nearby U.S. Navy Construction Battalion compound.

Not one soldier had been killed, although several were wounded, one seriously. That one was Private First Class David Hart. It was truely a miracle that he was still alive.

Everyone in the 1st Cav base was awake now and moving around like bees in a hive that had just been disturbed. The attack had only lasted about a minute but the explosions from ammo cooking off at the munitions storage area would continue well after dawn. Everything had not blown up in the initial explosion, so there was still a threat of more casualties and destruction.

Those troops on perimeter defense duty prepared for a possible follow-up ground attack. They fired some flares over the surrounding areas and lit up the night sky. The enemy, however, was long gone. They had set the timers on the rockets and then stealthly left the area. Typical. A lot of times the VC would do things like that just to cause some damage and casualties, with no intention of trying to overrun the base. They hadn't attempted that here since their big Tet Offensive in 1968.

Medics searched their areas of responsibility for casualties while other troops walked around to assess the damage done to facilities and equipment. It didn't take very long to discover the few men who'd been wounded in the attack. In most cases, calls of "Medic! Medic! Over here!" guided them to those in need of medical attention.

The first medic that came upon Hart's prone form, looked down at him and said to himself, "Oh shit, this ain't good." Even in the semi-darkness of lights from flares and flashlights, he could see this was a seriously bad case. It was clear that PFC Hart would need special medical care that was not available at either the 1st Cav or the Bien Hoa Air Base medical clinics. Luckily for him, there were medevac helicopters right here on this base.

The medics in the clinic had PFC Hart cleaned

up some, slowed the bleeding with heavy bandages and had some fresh blood flowing into his left arm within the ten minutes it took for the medevac chopper and crew to be ready for lift-off.

Several hours later and thousands of miles away in the small town of Darien, a few miles northeast of Stamford, Connecticut near Long Island Sound, Dora Hart woke up with a start. She was screaming out the name of her only son, David. Sitting up in bed, sweat beading on her face and soaking her nightgown, pillow case and sheets, she kept yelling, "David, David, come back!"

Ethan, her husband, woke up, startled by her sudden emotional outburst. He quickly reached over to his right and turned on the small lamp on the nightstand. The sight of his wife in her unkempt appearance and frightful expression that changed her pretty face into an almost unrecognizable person, shocked him.

Still half asleep and acting on instinct, he grabbed both of her upper arms and shook her a few times. He thought she'd been having a nightmare and a few shakes would wake her up before she woke up their sixteen-year-old daughter, Jennifer, asleep in the next room.

Dora **was** having a nightmare. It was about her son, David, getting killed in Vietnam. He'd been drafted into the Army and she had pleaded with him to try and get a job that would keep him out of combat, but to no avail.

His letters tried to reassure her that he was OK and that she shouldn't worry. But she was a mother and he was her child. Of course she would worry, it was only natural. That's what mothers do.

Even in her sleep, she could **feel** him

slipping away. It all seemed so real. She heard him calling out to her, "Moma, Moma!" in an almost child-like voice.

She cried out, "David, come back!" one last time before being brought back to the world of the living by a slap on her right cheek.

She took a deep breath, held it for a moment as tears rolled down her cheeks, then sighed so loudly that it shook Ethan to the very core of his being. It sounded like the death rattle of his grandmother that he'd heard a few years ago. He and some of his relatives were at her bedside when her long life came to an end. He never forgot that sound.

The familiar sound his wife just made, sent shivers through his whole body and he began to sob too, and he hugged her tightly for several minutes. As he held her in his arms with his chin on her right shoulder and his face pressed up against the side of her head, her entire body shook once and then she began to cry uncontrollably. Ethan prayed to God that it was only a nightmare and nothing more. He feared for his son's life as well.

At that very instant, half a world away, twenty-year-old PFC David Hart went into cardiac arrest. Tears rolled down his cheeks, this time real tears instead of blood, as he mentally cried out, "Moma, Moma!" Then there was that bright white light again, no rocket explosion this time, followed by eternal peace.

Try as they might, the doctors and nurses in the big Army 3rd Field Hospital in Saigon, just couldn't get his heart to start beating again. They thought his surgery, the first of several he would need, had been successful.

He was in a recovery room, closely monitored by both humans and the machines he was hooked up to.

They had already scheduled him to be flown on an Air Force C-9 Nightingale medical evacuation flight a couple of days from now. He was going to be transferred to the big 13th Air Force Regional Medical Center at Clark Air Base in the Philippines, only a two-hour flight from Tan Son Nhut Air Base in Saigon. There, he'd have more surgery performed on his face. They would attempt to make him look normal again and be able to function normally again too.

PFC Hart would still be flown from Vietnam to Clark Air Base, just not as a patient. Now he'd be making the trip inside of a metal coffin, another casualty in this seemingly endless war.

When the big silver C-141 Starlifter transport plane touched down on the single runway that had served Clark Air Base for many years, the Security Police Customs Section was notified. It had now become standard operating proceedures for each and every aircraft arriving from other bases in Southeast Asia, to be thoroughly searched by the SP's highly trained drug sniffing dogs. That included everything belonging to the flight crew. In fact, the crew wasn't allowed to get on the blue crew truck that regularly picked them up at their planes, until the ranking on-site security police team leader told them they were cleared to go.

The flight crew could thank some of their predecessors for this inconvenience. Some had been caught either trying to transport drugs in their personal baggage or inside of souvenirs. One of the most popular souvenirs from Thailand and South Vietnam at the time were knee-high ceramic elephants that some people used as potted plant stands. Their centers were hollow, so some ended up being used like a "Trojan horse," an innocent-looking piece of decorative artwork on the outside, a place to stash a few bags of heroin or marijuana on the inside. Several drug-filled ceramic elephants had already been discovered at Clark Air Base. Some drugs had also been found hidden in the cargo on some planes, including some caskets containing human remains.

This particular C-141 was transporting three metal caskets with the remains of three deceased American servicemen. It also had three pallets of damaged cargo pallets that were chained together and stacked six feet high and one pallet of regular mail.

The entire load was destined for Travis Air Force Base, California. It was the home base for the plane and crew, members of the 60th Military Airlift Wing. The unit was a part of Military Airlift Command. Back when the thirty-eight-year-old pilot first began flying, it was called Military Air Transport Service.

The SP dog handler led his pooch slowly around each of the metal caskets, allowing for some slack in the leash. The one containing Private First Class David Hart of Darien, Connecticut, was cleared first, quickly followed by the other two. The entire plane and all of its contents was declared "clean" in less than ten minutes. Then the crew was told that they were cleared to leave.

This former drug pipeline from Thailand and South Vietnam, through the Philippines, and back to the United States, was now running dry. It seemed that the U.S. President's silent war on drugs was beginning to win some battles.

The death of Private First Class David Hart was much more than just one more name added to the 58,000 others on a future monument. His death, like all the others that were a result of the Vietnam War, had a ripple effect. The lives of his parents, sister, grandparents, uncles, aunts, cousins, friends and fellow soldiers would never be the same.

CHAPTER 18

   The Cholon police chief's job came with a
very high price tag. It was the highest
priced job known to be for sale in South
Vietnam. By 1972 it cost $100,000. to the
major or lieutenant colonel who could raise
the cash to buy it. The previous chief was
in jail, having been found guilty of rape
and theft. He was lucky to be alive because
the older brother of the young woman he
raped had gone after him in the courtroom
with a knife. The young man had planned on
castrating the top cop.
   It only took a few months on the job for
the new police chief to recoup the money
spent and make about $50,000. a month by en-
gaging in shakedown rackets. Police protection was offered to businesses for a fee.
The Chinese businessmen in Cholon would
rather pay than be made to fight in the war
or try to fight against corruption in city
hall.
   The latest police chief, the sixth one in
the last ten years, was the oldest son of
Brigadier General Minh Vinh Giang. The general was a member of the South Vietnamese

Army Joint General Staff and a secret supporter of the Viet Cong. The son, "Little Tran" as he was called behind his back, was barely five feet tall but because of his rank of Major and the fact that his father was a Brigadier General in an important position, gave him an edge to get the job. The money was loaned to him by a friend of his father, Mang Binh Hao.

Little Tran was advised by Hao to turn a blind eye to the fact that the Viet Cong's C-10 Sapper Battalion was operating out of Cholon. If he left them alone, they'd leave him alone. That's how deals were done sometimes to keep the peace and survive.

The C-10 unit had been ordered to blow up the main building in the compound of the United States Information Service at 8 Le Qui Don Street. If they weren't able to do that, their alternate target was 6E Tu Xuong Street, where Charles Armstrong, the man in charge of the USIS lived. His residence was not far from his office in the USIS compound.

The compound was only about three blocks from the Presidential Palace and because of the close proximity, the deed would have to be done in the middle of a dark night. There were guards and government troops all around this part of town.

The task of the United States Information Service was to push the American line (aka propaganda) and provide easy access to American officials for the opinion formers working in the press corps. They gathered information about Viet Cong atrocities to use as anti-Communist propaganda. It was a branch of the U.S. Embassy and had become a thorn in the side of the Viet Cong.

While NVA forces engaged in large-scale battles against South Vietnamese forces during the Easter Offensive, the VC took on targets such as the USIS facility and American bases that were still in operation in the country. For reasons unknown to the VC, security around the USIS compound was increased shortly before their scheduled attack. They blew up the residence of the man in charge instead, killing a security guard and his live-in housemaid. By pure coincidence, Mr. Armstrong was in the President Hotel that night, cuddled up with one of the young women who worked there. The President Hotel was also frequented by lots of Navy SEALS whenever they were in Saigon. This was a war full of coincidences.

When the North Vietnamese Easter Offensive began, surprise was on their side. The large numbers of tanks and heavy artillery caught the South Vietnamese Army off guard. The NVA T-54 tanks were an even match for the ARVN's M-48 tanks. The NVA used their heavy artillery more than anything else to gain the advantage on the battlefields around Quang Tri City in the north, the city of Kontum in the central highlands and the city of An Loc, northwest of Saigon.

ARVN units around An Loc were initially supplied by truck convoys and helicopters. The Vietnamese 237th Helicopter Squadron, assisted by American UH1H Hueys and CH-47 Chinook twin-rotor, heavy-lift helicopters did all they could do until the anti-aircraft fire made it impossible to land supplies in An Loc. The NVA brought in .51 caliber and 37mm anti-aircraft guns and hand-launched, surface-to-air SA-7 Strela guided missles, destroying and damaging dozens of helicopters.

Once the NVA anti-aircraft fire got so bad that helicopters couldn't land on the battlefield with much-needed supplies anymore, American advisors called for cargo planes to air drop supplies to the beleaguered troops. To some of the Army old-timers, it reminded them of Bastogne during the Battle of the Bulge in World War II.

U.S. Air Force C-130 Hercules, Vietnamese Air Force C-123 Providers and their C-119 Flying Boxcar transport planes all answered the call for help. The 374th Tactical Airlift Wing and their Lockheed C-130s flew most of the missions and suffered the most losses. An Loc had no airfield so all the supplies needed had to be delivered by parachute.

South Vietnamese aircrews had been trained in conventional, daylight airdrop tactics, approaching the drop zones as low as 700 feet. The NVA gunners found easy targets at that altitude and so the South Vietnamese Air Force needed the help of American C-130s to keep their surrounded troops supplied. The American aircrews were trained in several airdrop tactics, including night drops. That scenario was repeated at Quang Tri and Kontum as well.

Because of the heavy anti-aircraft fire put up by NVA troops around An Loc, the USAF C-130 pilots had to use several different airdrop methods in both daylight and night missions. The NVA were able to shoot down three C-130s and two C-123s. They damaged dozens of other aircraft, killing and wounding several aircrew members who valiantly flew the dangerous resupply missions.

The anti-aircraft fire was so bad, many aircrew members resorted to wearing helmets and flackjackets for protection. Some of the loadmasters put tie-down chains inside of trash cans in the cargo compartment and then stood inside the trash cans. The term "trash haulers" took on a whole new meaning.

Most of the planes that flew the supply missions over the battlefields of An Loc took off from Tan Son Nhut Air Base in Saigon and Bien Hoa Air Base, about 18 miles northeast of

Saigon. Many fighterbombers from both the American and South Vietnamese Air Forces flew missions in support of the battle from those two bases as well. Things got so bad, a Marine squadron of A-4 Skyhawks and all their support personnel were sent from their base in Iwakuni, Japan to Bien Hoa to help out. An Loc was one of the most heavily contested battles of the war.

If NVA tanks had been able to travel down the road going southeast from An Loc, they could have been in Saigon in a matter of hours. That was one reason it was such a critical battle during the Easter Offensive.

The battle for Kontum wasn't going well for the South Vietnamese either. NVA forces did the same thing there. They pounded the city and military positions in the area with heavy artillery and then attacked with many tanks and supporting infantry. As the city was being surrounded, they brought in a lot of anti-aircraft weapons just as they had done at An Loc.

The main difference between Kontum and An Loc was that Kontum had an airfield. Three VNAF C-123 Providers that were used to bring in supplies and troops were damaged so badly after being hit by NVA shelling while parked on the airfield, all three had to be bulldozed off the aircraft parking ramp to make room for more transport planes arriving with badly needed supplies. One USAF C-130 was damaged so badly by enemy anti-aircraft fire that it crash-landed and was beyond repair. At least the crew managed to survive to fly another day. Eventually, Kontum had to depend solely on air-dropped supplies as the enemy surrounded it.

NVA forces, led by scores of tanks and heavy artillery, took over the city of Quang Tri. The ferocious fighting and the battle to re-take it cost both sides many casualties. Because of its location near the South China Sea, U.S. Navy ships were involved in the battle and destroyed some tanks, artillery pieces and troop concentrations. American advisors to the ARVN units used their communications equipment to call in fire missions for the Navy ships. They acted as spotters, along with slow flying O-1 Bird Dog spotter planes that carried an artillery liason/spotter along with the pilot to tell the Navy gunners if they hit their targets or not. They would assist the gunners in adjusting their fire when necessary.

As in the battles for Kontum and An Loc, some ARVN units around Quang Tri City had to receive air-dropped supplies to stay in the fight. NVA anti-aircraft fire destroyed one VNAF C-123 Provider and damaged several others, along with several helicopters.

American B-52 bombers increased their bombing missions inside of South Vietnam, flying from bases in Thailand and Guam. Fighter-bombers flown by USAF, Navy and Marine pilots flew many dangerous missions in support of the battling ARVN forces too. Every air base in South Vietnam and the aircraft carriers in the South China Sea were called upon to help stop the three-pronged invasion by NVA forces during the Easter Offensive. Airpower played a major role in stopping the enemy advance, causing them thousands of casualties and the loss of much-needed military equipment that had been transported on the ground all the way from North Vietnam. Without a doubt, it was the air-dropped supplies that kept the South Vietnamese soldiers and their American advisors in the fight, one that lasted until the third week of October.

The Ho Chi Minh Trail that began in western North Vietnam and ended southwest of An Loc was bombed more than ever before since it was used to transfer troops and supplies to South Vietnam. The bombings along the trail also affected the drug trade. The opium and marijuana that ended up in the hands of drug dealers in South Vietnam had to be transported through some of the areas of Laos and Cambodia that were bombed by American aircraft. Only a portion of the drugs grown in the Golden Triangle were transported by sea. The man who, more than anyone else, noticed this side-effect of the Easter Offensive was Mang Binh Hao.

The worldwide demand for drugs was steadily increasing but now the supply was steadily decreasing, resulting in higher prices. That fact helped Hao to make more money as time went on and the supplies continued to dwindle.

He made up for his drug trade losses by selling more scrap metal. South Vietnamese military forces lost more helicopters, planes, tanks, armored personnel carriers, trucks and jeeps during the Easter Offensive battles than they had in the previous three years all together. That created a lot of scrap metal, tons upon tons of it.

President Trung Ho Quoch made sure his generals removed the damaged and destroyed military equipment and empty artillery shell casings from the battlefields once things settled down. Most of the scrap metal ended up on Hao's ships and Quoch made millions on his kickback scheme.

President Quoch also had two of his generals removed from the battlefield as well. During the battle for An Loc, the ARVN 25th Division was ordered to send reinforcements there. General Van Nguyen Hoa was in command of the 25th, headquartered just a few miles northwest of Saigon. A couple of days later,

THE SAGE OF SAIGON

General Duong Pham Diem, commander of the ARVN 5th Division, which was headquartered only a few miles directly north of the capital, was also ordered to send reinforcements to the beleaguered troops surrounded at An Loc. Both generals had made a lot of money by padding their division payrolls with phantom soldiers, putting the pay of soldiers that didn't exist, into their bank accounts. Because of that, it was thought that their forces were much stronger than they actually were.

The deployment of the two army divisions to the battlefield resulted in very little change to the continued fighting. President Quoch and Lieutenant General Tan Pham Huu, the president's security advisor and senior military aide, traveled to the battlefield by helicopter to see for themselves. They both thought that the two additional divisions would turn the tide of battle in favor of ARVN forces. They were disappointed at what they saw.

After flying over the battlefield and talking to troops on the ground, they flew to both division headquarters. There they found the two cowardly commanding generals leading their troops from the safety of their air conditioned offices. After a quick question and answer session, both generals were fired and sent to Saigon in disgrace, placed under house arrest.

Neither one was ever charged with selling rice to the Viet Cong, selling military equipment provided by the U.S. government on the black market or of selling deferments from duty, things they had both done since taking command of their respective Army divisions. Had they been in the German army during WW II, they probably would have been put up against a wall and shot. But this was Vietnam and a very different kind of war.

Henri Ferrand sat in his office with his boss, Mang Binh Hao. He'd felt strong enough to come in and clean out all of his personal things after offering his resignation. There were few days now when he could even get up and walk around his house, much less do anything else. His nervous system was slowly shutting down.

Hao looked very sad as he sat there, looking across the old oak desk at a man he'd known for over twenty years. He could see a big difference in how Henri looked now compared to the day he was first informed about his tumor. He really looked terrible, so frail for a man his age. He actually felt very sorry for Henri. Henri was a good man.

"Henri, I feel sorry doctor can do nothing more for you. If I can do something, I do for you. You tell me, OK?"

"Merci beaucoup. I'm afraid there is nothing anyone can do for me. All I can do now is go home and live out my last days and be thankful to God for everything he gave me in this life." Well, there is one thing you can do for me, you sonofabitch, he thought. You can go to hell, you and all your cronies.

Hao stood up and told Henri in his own language this time, "Cam on ong, Henri," and reached out to shake his hand. "Thank you for everything you did to help this company. Goodbye." He couldn't help but notice how feeble Henri's handshake was, thinking it was due to his worsening condition.

As Hao walked down the hall towards the stairs leading down to the first floor, he made a mental note to have Henri and his daughter followed and watched carefully. Henri knew too much about his business and was still a liability as long as he lived. Hao knew how to deal with loose ends.

Henri began packing the well-hidden journals

into the empty cardboard boxes he'd brought with him that morning. Then he placed several miscellaneous items from his desk and some small framed pictures on top of the journals, making sure that nobody could see them. For all he knew, Hao might ask some of the employees what he took home with him. He couldn't afford to take any chances for these journals to be seen. He had one of the employees carry the boxes from his office to the taxi parked near the front door.

By the time he got home, Henri was wore out. It didn't take much of anything anymore to drain what little energy he had left. His housemaid and the taxi driver carried the boxes of stuff into the house for him.

After resting for a few minutes, he had Mai deliver a message to Genevieve. He wanted her to bring Lieutenant Ross over for another visit. Henri had decided on his next, and possibly his last, course of action.

CHAPTER 19

Ross and Genevieve were sprawled out on her bed, **their** bed now that he'd moved in with her. They had taken their relationship to the next level. It was bound to happen sooner or later as they were so attracted to eachother. The ceiling fan helped dry off their sweaty bodies as they rested, both naked and face-up, still breathing hard following an impromptu love-making session. There had been thunder inside the room to go with nature's thunder outside.

The rainy season had arrived and every day around noon the rains poured down. The temperature and humidity combined made a person perspire a lot, regardless of the rain. The air only cooled down a few degrees but remained very humid so even if you didn't get soaked from the rain, you never really felt totally dry, day or night.

Ross had to shine his uniform shoes and boots almost every day or they'd start turning green from mold. His web belts and wheel hat would turn green too if not cleaned frequently. He rarely wore them but he still had to keep them in good condition. He had to leave some of his things in the billet downtown to give the impression that he still lived there. He wasn't authorized to live in the apartment rented by Genevieve, so he went to his room in the billet every now and then just for appearances.

He looked to his right and stared at the framed 8" X 10" color picture of Genevieve's mother. There were several incense sticks burning in front of it, thin whisps of smoke drifting upwards from each one, then being blended together higher up by the ceiling fan and the small fan in the window. A small table was used to hold the items that turned that corner of the room into a small religious shrine of sorts.

Every once in awhile Ross could smell the fragrance of sandalwood that emanated from the burning incense. It reminded him of the joss sticks he'd seen in a Chinese Buddhist temple and the small candles lit at the front of the Catholic cathedral he'd gone into during a tour of Saigon and Cholon with Genevieve.

He turned in the opposite direction and focused his eyes on the amazingly beautiful female form, naked in the bed next to him. His eyes traced over the soft lines across her hills and valleys from head to toe as if he was studying a contour map on a field training exercise. The topography of this lovely female excited him much more than any map he'd ever seen. Much, much more.

The turn of her head towards him, followed by a warm smile caused him to ask himself a question. How is it that women can sense when a man is staring at them? Then she softly kissed him and gave his hand a firm squeeze. He took that as a good sign. Their relationship was still new and he had much to learn about her. He wasn't yet aware that, in their society, Vietnamese women were almost totally subordinate to men. Even though Genevieve was half-French and half-Vietnamese, she lived by what her mother had taught her. Treat your man well. He will return the good treatment generously.

"Are you OK?" he asked, barely above a whisper.

"Yes, of course. Are you?"

"No," he teased.

She suddenly looked worried and confused all at the same time.

"Is there something wrong?" she asked, with a discernible amount of concern in her voice.

"I'm not OK, I'm **fantastic**!" he said, now with a big grin on his face.

"Oh you! Do not tease me like that!" she said with a stern look.

He gave her a hug and a peck on the cheek and told her, "OK, I'm sorry, but it's true. I **do** feel fantastic. Being with you is a whole lot better than just 'OK'."

Ross pointed at the table with the burning incense and asked, "Was your mother Buddhist?"

"Yes, and also Confucianist."

"What about your father?"

"He is Protestant."

"How about you?" he wondered.

"Buddhist, Confucianist and Catholic," she replied, knowing that he wouldn't understand.

"How can you be Buddhist, Confucianist and Catholic all at the same time? I don't understand. Catholics are Christians but Buddhists and Confucionists are not, right?"

He knew a little bit about Catholics and Buddhists but hardly anything about Confucianists. And, he'd never heard of anyone being all three. This was new territory for him. His parents were Baptists and that's what was stamped on his dog tags, along with other things like his name and blood type. He wasn't a church goer anymore but he believed in God and did his praying in private.

"I will try to explain," she said as she sat up in bed.

His eyes briefly went from her face to her breasts, something he couldn't help if his life depended on it. Then they shifted back up before she could say, "Hey, I'm up here!" Damn, but she was beautiful, every inch of her. And her inches were all in the right places too.

"I went to a Catholic school from the time I was six until I graduated from high school. What I know about being Catholic, I learned from the nuns who were my teachers. What I know about Buddhism and Confucianism, I learned from my mother. She taught me about Vietnamese customs and culture too. Instead of saying one religion is right and the others all wrong, my mother told me that Vietnamese believe that one is right and another is not wrong either. In Vietnam, Christ, Mohammed, Buddha and Confucius may all be honored in the same temple. You can be both Buddhist and something else at the same time. Just like I learned in school about America, about freedom of religion, we have that too in Vietnam. So to honor my mother and her family, my Vietnamese ancestors, I am Buddhist and Confucianist. To honor my father's wishes for me to have a good education and be a Christian, I am also Catholic."

Genevieve had spoken as if she was a teacher in a classroom, feeling like she'd done a pretty good job of explaining things. She had kept her lesson simple for him, hoping that he wouldn't distance himself because of her beliefs.

Ross told her, "I've seen Buddhist monks on TV and seen statues of Buddha and stuff but I'm not sure what a Confucianist is. Is that religion related to the Chinese guy named Confucius?" About that religion, he really was that naive.

He turned over onto his left side and softly ran the fingertips of his right hand along the top of her smooth thigh, delighting at the feel of her soft skin. She promptly swatted his hand away. Now he was being an irreverent student. His hand stung a little. Be cool, man. There's plenty of time for that later. Pay attention now, his inner voice told him.

Genevieve used the same hand she'd just used to swat his hand with and gently, lovingly, caressed the back of his head and neck. Patting a person on the top of their head is considered an insult in Vietnamese culture and she purposefully avoided putting her hand there. Then she began with her explanation of Confucianism, hoping again that he would be accepting of her multi-religious beliefs.

Remembering how the nuns had taught class, she began with simple facts. "The Chinese brought the philosophy, taught by Confucius, to Vietnam many centuries ago. It is like a moral code about relations between people like father and son, wife and husband, young people to old people, friend to friend. Achievement of harmony is the first duty of every Confucianist. Then, after a Confucianist dies, they are revered as an ancestor who is joined to nature forever. The dead person's children honor and preserve their memory. That is what I do with my mother now, burning incense in front of her picture. I tell her what I do and ask for her advice about things. I saw on TV one time, an American man visiting his dead wife in a cemetery. He brought her flowers and talked to her even though she was dead. So you see, it is the same thing I do here. Everyone does essentially the same thing, but in a slightly different way. Under our skin, in our hearts, we are all the same. More the same than we sometimes realize, right? You understand better now?" she concluded.

"Yeah, I think so. That explains why you are so nice to be with. Your religion is a part of you, a part of who you are and," he added after a brief pause, "I really love the person you are."

He reached behind his head where she'd placed a hand and brought it around to his lips. He kissed her hand and then laced his fingers between hers and kissed the back of her hand again. It was so much smaller than his and a lot softer too. He looked into her slightly almond-shaped, not-quite-round, dark brown eyes and she looked right into his. Neither one said a word as they embraced and kissed, tenderly at first, then passionately. The loud thunder from the storm outside covered up the sounds they began making with their own thunderous fireworks display inside.

Sunday started out just like the stormy day before had, sunny, hot and steamy. All the rain from the day before had created puddles of water everywhere and it only added to the already high levels of humidity. Ross sometimes worked on weekends but not this one.

Genevieve was just outside their apartment entrance, playing mahjong with three other women from the building. The balcony-like walkway that led to their apartment door was just wide enough to accommodate the 144 tiles and the women as they played the game of Chinese origin.

On his days off, Ross usually lounged around in a white T-shirt and cut-off blue jean shorts, especially if they weren't going anywhere. That's what he was wearing now as he watched the women for a few minutes. He wondered how they could read the black characters printed on the white mahjong pieces. They looked like Chinese characters to him. Had they been Japanese or Korean, he probably wouldn't have known the difference. He was surprised at just how many different things in Vietnam that had Chinese origins.

Genevieve didn't say anything to him when she noticed him standing nearby. She just looked up at him and smiled, the kind that melts men's hearts, at least his anyway. He smiled back then walked away.

He went back inside the apartment and went to the window that overlooked the narrow street below. Seconds before, a jeep full of Vietnamese police had pulled up and the ranking member of the group was shouting out orders as his men entered the building. Ross kept watching out of curiosity. It had been a peaceful, quiet day until now.

The women playing mahjong started talking excitedly and louder than before. They quickly threw all the mahjong tiles into an apron held out by one of the women. Then they ran down the stairs to their respective apartments as if they feared that something bad was about to happen. They were all barefooted and made hardly a sound as they ran from the sunny walkway to the darker stairwell below.

When Ross heard the chattering of excited voices behind him, he turned around just in time to see Genevieve run back inside. She locked the door and told him to run into the bathroom and not make a sound. She had a look of fear in her face. He knew something wasn't right.

When they were standing in the shower with the bathroom door locked, Ross looked at the light green housedress made of lightweight cotton that accentuated Genevieve's nice figure.

Those were her every day clothes when staying home and she knew that Ross liked the way they looked on her too.

Ross whispered, "What's going on?"

"The police are here," she began, "and they are looking for military deserters. That is what they tell everyone. What they really want is money. If you give them money they will not mess up your house when they look for deserters."

"Well, I'm not a deserter." Ross declared. "Why should we hide from them? I'll just tell them to go away."

"No! You cannot do that!" Genevieve reproached adamantly. "They will ask us for marriage papers. If they find us together with no papers, they will arrest me for prostitution and put me in jail."

"They can't do that!" Ross stated a little too loudly.

Genevieve put a hand over his mouth and shushed him. Then she explained, "The police here can do anything they want. They can put you in jail too if you do not give them money. No more talking now so I can listen!" she hissed at him.

He remained silent for the next few minutes as they both strained to hear the voices coming from the stairwell below. Muffled voices came from different areas of the building as the police shakedown, on the pretense of looking for deserters, continued.

While nobody had yet knocked on their door, they were both still worried that they might be discovered. They could hear a woman talking, then pleading and crying loudly out in the street. The crying didn't stop until the police left.

Once the police were gone, Genevieve told Ross it was OK for them to leave the bathroom. She then went downstairs for a few minutes to check with some of the other tenants to find out what happened. One of the women she'd been playing mahjong with told her that the police didn't realize that she and her American boyfriend lived in an apartment with an outside entrance. They only checked the apartments that had an entrance in the main stairwell.

The woman crying out in the street was upset because she didn't have enough money to satisfy the police and keep them from trashing her apartment while looking for alledged military deserters. It would take hours for her and her family to clean up the mess the police left behind.

The most disturbing news that Genevieve shared with Ross later was what one of the mahjong players overheard one of the policemen telling another one. He told one of the others to keep an eye out for the Frenchman's daughter, that Mang Binh Hao would reward them handsomely for information about her whereabouts.

The lease on her apartment was not up yet but they had to move **now**.

CHAPTER 20

There was no moon on this still, warm and muggy night and the stars in the darkened sky appeared as bright as ever. It was a perfectly dark and peaceful night for sleeping, at least for most people.
BOOOOM! The loud explosion woke up the South Vietnamese sentries that had been vigilantly guarding a portion of their section of the Bien Hoa Air Base perimeter before they both fell asleep. The bright flash of light and the loud explosion was less than fifty feet from their sandbagged position.
Before they realized exactly what had happened, a much bigger and louder explosion came from behind them, causing them to think that a rocket or mortar attack was taking place. They looked at eachother with wide-eyed fear and crouched down in their guard-post position as low as they could possibly get. A long period of silence followed, with only the buzzing of mosquitoes near their ears in the humid, breezeless night air, the only sound to be heard. They stayed cowering in fear until their watch captain showed up behind them in his jeep, demanding to know

what happened.

Before either of the men answered, the radioman in the captain's jeep handed him the radio handset. After a brief back-and-forth conversation, he ordered the two sentries to fire some flares.

"We've been attacked by sappers," he told them. "Stay alert!" he ordered.

Daylight revealed the damage to both men and materials. The first explosion that night had killed one of the two members of the Viet Cong's C-10 Sapper Battalion that operated around Saigon, Long Binh and Bien Hoa.

On his way into the base, the sapper had somehow managed to crawl through several rows of concertina wire, trip-flares and Claymore mines undetected and unscathed.

He and his accomplice had stealthily set their satchel charges next to a large warehouse on the Vietnamese side of the base. Then they made their way back to the entry point on the perimeter of the base without being seen. On the way back through the rows of concertina wire, trip-flares and Claymore mines, the unfortunate VC sapper touched the trip wire of a mine with just enough pressure to set it off. The second explosion had been the warehouse being destroyed by their satchel charges.

There wasn't much left of the dead VC after the mine exploded. Hundreds of tiny steel ball bearings blasted through the thin plastic covering of the mine and put more holes in him than a piece of Swiss cheese. It wasn't pretty. The mine was set up at ground level, with the curved concave side facing towards the base. The curved convex side that had the words stamped into it, telling the user to point this side towards the enemy, was pointing away from the base. Instead of a wire attached to it and connected to a detonator box powered by a half-volt battery, allowing the user to press a clacker and setting off the mine, the wire from this Claymore went to a small steel rod that was pushed into the ground. One tug on that wire and BOOOOM! Lights out Charlie!

The other member of the C-10 Sapper Battalion survived and made a clean get-away. Liberation Radio, the Viet Cong's AM radio propaganda station, sang their praises the next day. As always, they blew the story way out of proportion. According to their claims, several "puppet soldiers" of the South Vietnamese Air Force (VNAF) were killed and three vintage Korean War-era A-1 Skyraiders that were being repaired in the building that was "totally destroyed and burned to the ground," were added to their claims.

In truth, the storage warehouse that belonged to the VNAF Air Logistics Command, contained only parts for various types of helicopters and planes, never any complete aircraft. Neither VNAF nor any American servicemen suffered any casualties. There was only the embarassment of not noticing two VC sappers crawling within fifty feet of the perimeter guards that caused any amount of suffering. Sleeping while on guard duty carried a stiff penalty.

The VC were also making plans involving Saigon and the sprawling Long Binh Army Base. Their little foray into Bien Hoa was done just to let everyone know that they could strike anywhere at any time. 1968 had been a very bad year for them. Now they were getting stronger again, with more financial means to buy weapons and with more replacements of cadre to help free their land from those who opposed their struggle to unite it as one country once again. Time and willpower were on their side and they knew it.

The VC attacks were timed to coincide with the offensive led by the North Vietnamese Army. This time, however, they'd let their northern brothers lead the charge, for the most part. Instead of hoping for an uprising of the general population as they had in 1968, the plan for 1972 called for tank-led and artillery-supported attacks that pitted the NVA directly against the South Vietnamese Army. The Easter Offensive was that plan and it was taking a toll on U.S. and South Vietnemese forces.

CHAPTER 21

Henri was confused. He read every newspaper he could get his hands on each day, even the Pacific Stars And Stripes, the American newspaper printed in Japan and distributed all over Asia daily for U.S. military forces far from home. The newspaper articles said the U.S. president had visited China from February 21st through the 28th. He met with the Chinese Communist Party leader, hoping to reestablish diplomatic relations.
China had been supplying North Vietnam and Communist military forces in Laos and Cambodia with weapons and military advisors for years. Many South Vietnamese and American troops had been killed by those weapons.
At the same time the U.S. president was in China, his National Security Advisor was in Paris, France meeting with a delegation of North Vietnamese negotiators. They were working on the Paris Peace Accords, with the U.S. delegation hoping to find a peaceful end to the war in Vietnam.
The war had become very unpopular to a large segment of the American population, according to what Henri read in the papers

and heard on TV. Had the United States decided to betray their friends and allies and side with the Communists by giving in to their demands? Henri didn't know what to make of American politics. One thing was for certain though. These two much-publicized events really pissed off the president of South Vietnam.

Trung Ho Quoch felt betrayed, especially after finding out that the U.S. Congress was talking about cutting off all funding for the war. The pressure on President Trung Ho Quoch was mounting and he was now speaking out publicly about it.

The pressure on Henri was mounting too. He was aware that Mang Binh Hao was paying people to find his daughter. Had Hao found out that he was being investigated by Bui Van Nha of the Vietnamese CIA? Had Hao found out that he had spoken with Nha on a few occasions and thought there was a connection? Hao knew where Henri lived and so far had left him alone.

But why? To do something to his beloved daughter instead? To get him to confess about his knowledge of Hao's dirty deeds and his powerful politically-connected friends who were also taking advantage of their positions to become filthy rich? The mere possibility that Hao would try to get to him through his daughter worried Henri a lot.

He knew his time left on earth was short. He made up his mind to do something to protect his daughter. He hoped she would forgive him if she ever found out.

He also finally decided to give the journals to someone who would find them useful. Someone who could actually **do** something with them.

Genevieve had received the invitation to

visit her father again shortly before she and Ross moved from their apartment. Now they were temporarily living in the Federal Hotel in Cholon. Their second floor room overlooked a narrow street in a neighborhood that was a mixture of small businesses and residences. Most of the buildings on this street were two and three-story structures containing many small apartments.

The Federal Hotel was built in the center of a row of these types of buildings. A few businesses that were still open operated on the ground floor. The owners usually lived right above them in the upstairs apartments. Most of the small, family-run businesses had accordian-like metal gates that could be stretched across the entire property, providing protection and security.

The average apartment in this part of town measured only ten feet wide and twenty feet long. They were often occupied by more than one family or several generations of the same one. The war had created a housing shortage due to the thousands of refugees that sought the relative safety of the big city.

Ross and Genevieve could look straight across the street from their room and see a family's laundry hung up to dry on a clothesline strung across their balcony. The Federal Hotel also had balconies for rooms on the second and third floors. They only ventured out on theirs at night for fear of being seen.

Each day Genevieve walked the short distance to a Chinese market around the corner and bought their meals. It was a variation of "Chinese take-out." She wanted Ross to try a meat and vegetable soup, similar to pho, but with little marble-sized meatballs in it. When he described it to his co-workers back at MACV, they jokingly told him it was monkey ball soup. Whatever it was, he liked it.

The TV in their hotel room didn't work very well. The old black and white set was in need of a new set of rabbit ears. The good news was, the window air conditioner would produce tiny ice pellets when turned up to full blast. Ross and Genevieve enjoyed the cool dry air it provided as well as another reason to snuggle up close in bed.

Whenever they were together, which was not every day due to his work schedule and having to visit other bases periodically, they spent many hours talking about everything young couples usually talk about. And they did what many couples their age did when staying together under this situation. They became very intimate, both physically and mentally. Their relationship developed into a typical wartime romance under not-so-typical circumstances.

On the evening of their visit to Genevieve's ailing father, they walked down the narrow street from their hotel and hailed a yellow and blue taxi that had just dropped off a passenger at a nearby intersection. The roads were still wet from the afternoon rain showers.

As the water evaporated, it formed a light fog close to the ground and they could see it in the headlights of their cab. Going from an air conditioned room to these conditions outdoors gave them the feel of entering a Finnish sauna. That's just the way things were in Saigon this time of the year. Air conditioning just made it that much more noticeable.

Genevieve was worried that her father may have taken a turn for the worse. The note Mai had brought to her didn't give a reason why her father wanted her and Ross to visit again. She knew there was no hope for his recovery but prayed to Jesus and Buddha every day for a miracle. She told Ross about her concerns. As they rode in the back seat of the taxi that evening, he tried to console her. He put an arm around her and his hand in hers, telling her to be strong and hope for the best.

    She'd already taught him about Vietnamese culture in regards to public displays of affection. He understood and respected them and confined his hugs or hand-holding to private settings like in the back of the taxi, out of public view. He was a fast learner. Plus, he made her feel safer by becoming her private bodyguard. What woman could not love a man like that?

    Once again, she and Ross were greeted at the door by Mai, her father's housemaid. After leading them into the house and announcing their arrival, she excused herself to prepare tea for everyone. As Genevieve had explained to Ross, tea was the principal Vietnamese beverage in the morning, afternoon and evening. It was served at all social gatherings like when visiting someone's home. He still preferred coffee over hot tea and once she confided in him that her father did too. Ross only wished ice tea would catch on here like it did back home. About the only place you could find ice tea in Vietnam was in a big restaurant or a military mess hall.

    When they entered the livingroom, they were surprised to see a woman sitting in a chair off to one side of Henri. Between them was a wheelchair. The lady was clearly Vietnamese, around Henri's age. She wore the white uniform of a nurse.

    "Bon soir, Papa," Genevieve greeted her father. Then she greeted the nurse in Vietnamese. "Chao ba."

Surprising both Ross and Genevieve, the nurse returned the greeting in Vietnamese and then spoke mostly in English.

"So, this is the trung uy (first lieutenant) your father speaks so highly of?"

"Yes. And do you also speak French?"

"Oui. However, I have been working with doctors from Australia and America in several new Rural Life Hamlets for a few years now and my English is now better than my French I think."

Henri cut in. "Miss Lee was recommended to me by a doctor friend of hers at the French-run Grall Hospital here in Saigon. He is also a good friend of my doctor. As you know, my brain tumor is slowly taking away my ability to do things for myself. I'm finding it hard to walk and maintain my balance. That is why the wheelchair is here. As time goes on, I will need to be administered higher doses of pain medication. My doctor advised me to find a nurse who can live here full-time to help me in the coming days. Miss Lee, please explain to my daughter and her friend where you used to work and why you are now available to help me. S'il vous plait."

Before she began, Mai entered the room and served them all tea. Then she excused herself and left the room but stayed close enough to the kitchen entrance to hear. She was curious to find out about this new female who would be living in the house.

Miss Lee took a sip of her tea and then began. "I was hired by the Vietnamese government to be a nurse in the new Rural Life Hamlet program several years ago. That was a program that was a part of the Rural Reconstruction or Pacification program. It was designed to provide physical safety, a strong local government and hopefully, a better life for the rural population, many of whom were poor rice farmers."

She paused just long enough to sip her tea again and looked the young American man over. Many of his kind had come here and died while trying to keep them free from a complete Communist takeover. While she admired them for that, she privately wished they'd leave the young women alone. She took a big breath and continued.

"Where I did most of my work was in small, sparsely populated hamlets that had only rudimentary fortifications. A few of the men were trained as militia by some American and South Vietnamese soldiers who spent only a few days visiting each hamlet. The men that were trained to use the guns supplied by the My, excuse me, the Americans, were mostly poor rice farmers who were not well educated. Sometimes they fought bravely against the Viet Cong and sometimes they just ran away."

Another pause, another sip of tea.

"The aid stations I worked at were set up in schools mostly and we treated people for many different things, fevers, burns, even wounds from punji sticks, land mines and from the fighting. Sometimes the government would supply us with medical supplies and most of it came from the United States. They also sent teachers, Agricultural Department people and sometimes American bac si, doctors, both military and civilian. They would stay and help us for a few days. The overall program goal was to keep as many people as possible loyal to the Saigon government and not to help the Viet Cong."

Miss Lee stopped again to sip some tea and then she looked over at Henri. When he nodded at her, she continued telling her story. The guests were eager to hear the rest of it. So was Mai.

"I had to leave the Rural Life Hamlet program because the Viet Cong killed some people just to show me what would happen to me if I did not leave."

She looked over at Henri again, appearing unsure if she should continue. He nodded at her to go ahead.

"One night they snuck into the hamlet chief's house. His only daughter and her husband lived with him and his wife. When the hamlet chief woke up in the morning, he found his son-in-law's head on the kitchen table. He screamed and ran into his daughter's room. There was a huge amount of blood all over the floor and he almost slipped and fell in it. Looking across the room, he saw his son-in-law's body, face-up, with his legs spread apart. In between his legs and pushed right up to his crotch was the head of his daughter. Her headless body was in bed next to her headless husband. Both had been stabbed many times. A note on the kitchen table warned the hamlet chief not to invite any government people to his hamlet ever again and warned all members of the medical team I was on to leave right away or we would be targeted next. We left that afternoon after helping bury the young couple."

Genevieve had her hand over her mouth and looked like she'd just seen a ghost. Ross sat next to her shaking his head back and forth in disbelief. Atrocities such as that always affected people when hearing them for the first time. The story was very upsetting and shocking to them both.

After a long silent minute in which no one spoke, Henri broke the uncomfortable silence.

"Do you see what we have to deal with, Tom? This is no ordinary war. And what I am going to tell you about it today may shock you some more. Do you have a few minutes?"

"Sure." He looked at Genevieve and she shook her head in the affirmative. He doubted that he could tell him anything that would shock him more than Miss Lee's story.

"I have been living in Vietnam since the late 1940s. I know these people and I know what they are capable of. Let me tell you about one of them."

"OK," Ross replied. He focused on Henri and sipped his tea in anticipation of a good story.

"Ho Chi Minh was born on May 19, 1890 in Annam. That's what the central part of Vietnam was called back then. As everyone now knows, he died on September 3, 1969. Do you know what his name at birth was?"

Ross was caught off guard, not expecting to be asked any questions during the storytelling. After a brief pause, he admitted, "No idea, Henri. Sorry."

Henri had thought correctly. Most people didn't.

"He was born Nguyen Tat Thanh. Do you know what Ho Chi Minh means?"

Again, Ross was taken by surprise. He just shrugged his shoulders and shook his head no.

"The Enlightener. He traveled to France after World War I and helped found the French Communist Party. That is why we French know so much about him. He used a different name back then instead of his own. He went by the name Nguyen Ai Quoc, which means Nguyen the Patriot. He later traveled to Moscow for training in Communist ideology."

He paused for a few seconds to sip some tea. His throat was getting dry from all this talking.

"After Russia, he traveled to China to organize the Communist Vietnamese who fled there from French Indochina. He was the founder of the Indochinese Communist Party. Then he returned to French Indochina and founded the

Viet Minh and fought against the Japanese in World War II. After the war, he changed his name from Nguyen Ai Quoc to Ho Chi Minh and created the Democratic Republic of Vietnam, with the goal of unifying the country. His forces defeated the French and the French military left Vietnam. Now the American military forces are leaving Vietnam after failing to defeat his Communist forces as well. Ho Chi Minh was born a lowly peasant and look at all that he accomplished."

Ross just sat there politely listening and nodding his head to show that he was paying attention. He wondered what all this was leading up to. He had to admit, he learned something new.

Henri continued. "You must learn about your enemies and know them well, Tom. The willpower of the Vietnamese Communists here and in the North will eventually overcome the willpower of the leaders of your country and South Vietnam. Mark my words young man. We French learned that the hard way. We lost over 35,000 killed and more than 48,000 wounded. It was also financially disastrous for our country too. From what I have observed, it seems that American politicians have learned nothing from history and are repeating it."

Henri would soon explain to Ross what that information he just gave him had to do with what he was about to propose.

"Genevieve my dear," he said as he stood up on unsteady legs, "please excuse Tom and I for a few minutes. We are going to the kitchen for a cup of coffee. I would like to speak to him in private. Don't worry, I won't keep him long," he said as he smiled, first at Ross, then at Genevieve.

Miss Lee stood up also and handed Henri his cane, now forced to use one because of his worsening condition. He slowly led Ross into the kitchen and instructed Mai to make them a pot of coffee. Genevieve had mentioned to him before that when she saw Ross drink coffee in the morning, it reminded her of him when she was a child. She had memories of her mother having tea while he had coffee in the morning.

When they were seated in the kitchen and sipping some really good coffee, Henri told Ross about the information Nha had shared with him. It included Nha's beliefs about the impending demise of South Vietnam. Then he really shocked him with the news of his journals, their specific contents and his plan.

CHAPTER 22

Captain Daniels and Lieutenant Ross were the only members of the 1st Special Investigations Unit invited to the JUSPAO building on Le Loi Boulevard in Saigon for this particular briefing. Daniel's boss, Lieutenant General Christianson, was conducting a part of the briefing.

The Joint U.S. Public Affairs Office was the official voice of MACV and was where the daily military press briefings known as the "Five O'clock Follies" were held. Civilian journalists had come up with that name for the briefings because they didn't believe half of what they were told. Briefing officers were from the various branches of the armed forces and today it was the Army's turn to "enlighten" the civilian journalists in attendance. The unusual thing about this briefing was, the MACV commander himself was one of the briefers.

Unknown to either Captain Daniels or Lieutenant Ross at this time was that their unit was about to be disbanded and all the investigators would return to the same types of investigative units they had originally come from. Assignment orders to a new base were in the works for them all, just a regular part of the U.S. withdrawal of military forces from South Vietnam, nothing out of the ordinary.

The invitation to the briefing came from the commanding general of MACV himself and neither Daniels nor Ross knew why they were singled out. All they were told was, wear some clean starched fatigues and shined boots and don't be late.

Apparently someone must have tipped off CBS News as to the identity of the main briefer because their shuttle bus from the Caravelle Hotel arrived early and their reporters all had front row seats for a change.

The Caravelle Hotel was built in the late 1950s and was known to have the coldest air conditioning system in all of Saigon. Air France was said to be one of the owners of the tall white stucco building. The rooms were the most expensive in the whole city.

Its wide spiral staircase that led to the second floor was used primarily by CBS News employees as that company rented most of its offices and rooms there.

General Christianson had never stayed in the Caravelle Hotel. He and other generals and senior colonels preferred the exclusive club at Le Cercle Sportif, another remnant of French colonial influence.

Captain Daniels and Lieutenant Ross both left the briefing in shock. Not only had the MACV commander introduced them to the journalists, he had bragged on the accomplishments of their unit, a unit once unknown to all but a few people and for a good reason.

While not naming any individuals from the journals he'd read, he told the news people about the joint investigation by both U.S. and South Vietnamese authorities into the graft and corruption revealed in the journals that were "discovered" by Lieutenant Ross during one of his investigations.

General Christianson was not aware of the deal that Ross had made with Henri to get the journals. That was something that Henri insisted that Ross swear to him, to never tell a soul, and especially not Genevieve, about their deal. Nobody would ever know that the journals and the marriage of Ross to Genevieve were in any way connected. That's exactly the way Henri wanted it. To insure that Ross went through with his part of the deal, Henri only gave him three of the six journals. When he was satisfied that the marriage had taken place and his daughter would be leaving South Vietnam and be out of danger, he would turn over the other three to Ross. He hoped to live that long.

Ross proposed to Genevieve one night when they were standing outside on the small balcony of their hotel room. They were looking up at the night sky and discussing the recent visit with her father.

"I see a bright star," he said.

"Where? I do not see any," she replied. Her eyes searched the sky for one. The city lights made it difficult to see any stars.

Ross reached into his pocket, brought out the small black velvet-covered box and opened it. Then he knelt down on one knee, holding the box with the diamond engagement ring up, about even with Genevieve's waist.

"It's right here. Look down here."

She turned and looked down at him, not understanding what was going on.

"Genevieve Ferrand, will you marry me and be my wife?"

Then it finally sank in. There was a ring

in the box, the bright star he had seen. She bent down, almost knocking him over as she hugged him tightly and said yes.

After he put the ring on her finger, she started sobbing tears of joy. She must have hugged Ross for five full minutes before letting him go. Their first kiss as an engaged couple lasted almost as long as the hug. It was the start of a beautiful night.

While Ross might have asked her to marry him sometime in the future, Genevieve's fate had been sealed by her father. She would never learn how that came about.

Her father had told her that he had a feeling that Ross was in love with her and he had been right. Ross was very much in love with this soon-to-be twenty, half-French, half-Vietnamese beauty. The marriage proposal just wouldn't have happened so soon had Henri not said a word to Ross about the journals.

Ross told her they needed to change into some nice clothes so they could go someplace special and celebrate their engagement.

"Where are we going?" she asked as she dried her eyes and tried to stop sobbing.

"A place someone told me about over on Tu Do Street."

"Are we going to a bar?"

"No, the Continental Palace Hotel. This is a special occasion so I'm taking you to a special place. We're going to spend the night there too so bring your toothbrush," he added.

They caught a taxi and in a few minutes they found themselves on a sidewalk, looking up at the 3-story hotel. The Continental Palace Hotel was built in the French colonial style around 1928. It had high ceilings, shuttered windows and a cool shaded courtyard in the center. It was the fanciest hotel either of them had ever been in. Once inside, they walked around with eyes wide open like little kids in a toy store, oohing and aahing at the beautiful decor they'd never seen before.

After the bellhop escorted them to their room, their amazement continued. The room had beautiful but very old French provincial furniture. There was cracked and peeling paint on all four walls which only enhanced the overall ambiance of the old French decor. There was a large ceiling fan over the king size bed. Their room had a high double window with wooden shutters that reminded Ross of some of the buildings he'd seen in New Orleans once.

The bathroom had tiled walls and a tiled floor. There was an antique enameled iron bathtub with shower. It also had a sink and French-style toilet with a bidet. You had to hand it to the French. When it came to personal hygiene, the bidet was their invention. Soft toilet paper was not though, Ross later discovered.

While Ross and Genevieve enjoyed their first meal together as an engaged couple, other Americans dined in Saigon that night in nice hotels across the city. The Caravelle, the Miramar, the Peninsular, the Majestic, the President and the Rex, with its open-air restaurant on the roof, all enjoyed a quiet respite from the war that raged around them in other parts of the country.

Ross was very busy over the next few days. He was required by military regulations to tell Captain Daniels about his intentions to marry Genevieve. His commander had to not only give him permission to marry a foreign national but provide some guidance on the matter and sign some forms, lots and lots of forms. The large amount of paperwork and the briefings, background checks and physical exams were all a part of the government's plan to make it a difficult and time-consuming process. The idea was that some GIs would give up in frustration. And some did. It was all tied in with immigration quotas and the U.S. government didn't want the GIs bringing in a flood of Asian brides into the country, some of whom could be undercover enemy agents or just out-and-out golddiggers, looking to use the naive and unsuspecting GI husbands as a free ride to the land of opportunity.

The screening process to eliminate that possibility was in place and Ross would have to endure a lot of frustration over the coming months as he attempted to get married, protect Genevieve by getting her out of the country and get his hands on the other three, and possibly, the most important journals of all.

Someone told him about a Vietnamese lawyer who, for a fee of a few hundred American dollars, would "grease the wheels" of a system of administration that was marked by officialism, red tape and good old fashioned greed. It seemed that every Vietnamese office in Saigon that a GI had to take his marriage paperwork to for an official stamp or raised seal and signature, there was someone with a hand out who wanted a gratuity. If they didn't receive one, the paperwork got delayed for any number of reasons and the GI told to return at a later date.

Ross hired the lawyer and hoped for the best.

Fire Base Crossed Sabers was one of dozens of firebases scattered across South Vietnam. It was only 42 miles east of Saigon and had been the location of Charlie Company, 1st Battalion, 7th Cavalry, 1st Cavalry Division. After they folded their flag and flew back to the land of the big PX, a South Vietnamese army unit took up positions there, enjoying the bunkers and sandbagged positions left behind by the Americans. They didn't stay very long.

Now those positions were temporarily occupied by the 33rd North Vietnamese Army Regiment. They had traveled long distances during the Easter Offensive and were now poised for a move towards the bases at Bien Hoa and Long Binh. Only a few miles southwest of them was the capital city of Saigon.

Only 17 miles north of Saigon were the hamlets of Xon Suoi, An Hoa and Thu Thanh. All three were captured by elements of three NVA regiments operating between Saigon and Ben Cat, 27 miles to the north. Because of the loss of those hamlets and others around Saigon, waves of B-52 bombers were used to blast NVA troop concentrations, some as close as 20 miles from the capital.

U.S. Marine Corps A-4 Skyhawk fighter/bombers attacked NVA positions only 15 miles north of Saigon and within 7 to 8 miles of their own base at Bien Hoa.

Some of the B-52 "Arc Light" missions flew close enough to Saigon and Bien Hoa to cause doors and windows to rattle from the concussion of thousands of exploding 750-pound bombs. It was during this turbulent and unpredictable period of the Communist Easter Offensive that Ross got orders sending him on a TDY, temporary duty to Detachment 5005 of the OSI unit at Bien Hoa Air Base. The detachment was being deactivated and its personnel sent back to the U.S.

Lieutenant Ross had a simple mission. Transport all the records in the office of Detachment 5005 to their sister OSI detachment at Tan Son Nhut Air Base. All of the OSI detachments scattered throughout South Vietnam were packing up and leaving. Ross just happened to be one of only a few people who had the proper security clearance to sign for the paperwork and was also temporarily free of other important duties to be gone from his own unit for 48 hours. All he had to do was drive a 3/4 ton truck from Saigon to Bien Hoa. A forklift would place the locked metal cabinets in the back of the truck for him.

Ross would spend the night in the Visiting Officers Quarters (VOQ) and then follow the Army's big green shuttle bus the next morning as it made stops at Bien Hoa, the Navy Seabee compound down the road just past the 1st Cav part of Bien Hoa, then on to USARV HQ at Long Binh Army Base. It would then go on to MACV HQ from there, right across the street from one of the gates at Tan Son Nhut Air Base.

It was always safer to travel with another military vehicle with armed personnel aboard. Ross had his .38 Special with him but that would be no match against an AK-47 should he have to defend himself.

When Ross told Genevieve about his upcoming 2-day TDY, she quickly arranged for a Buddhist good luck ceremony for him. They took a taxi from the Federal Hôtel to an unfamiliar part of Cholon, one that was crowded with poorly-built wood and tin buildings. She introduced Ross to the man who would perform the ceremony. He spoke no English at all so Genevieve did most of the talking and all of the interpreting.

"What kind of a place is this?" Ross asked as he took in the unusual sights.

The room they were in was like one giant Buddhist temple. There were several statues of a big, round-bellied Buddha, sitting with legs crossed and with many small children sitting all around. It reminded Ross of a happy grandfather being surrounded by many grandchildren at Christmas or some other special time. There were many incense sticks already lit and filled the room with the scent of sandalwood. Red and gold were the two dominating colors he noticed.

"This is a special place. Take off your boots and kneel down on the mat and face the large Buddha," Genevieve instructed. "Do not be afraid. He will touch both of your shoulders with the sword and pray to Buddha to protect you. Then he will give you a special cloth with some writing on it. Never show anyone that cloth. I am the only person who is allowed to see it because it is a special blessing for us. Now, bow your head."

Ross did as she instructed. He kept his eyes on the man who now had a big sword in his hands. He was chanting something and gently touched the flat side of the big sword on each of his shoulders. Ross felt like he was being knighted by a king, the only thing his mind could think of at the moment, something to compare this event to. He hoped the guy wasn't a VC with a strong dislike of Americans. He'd like to keep his head a little longer.

After setting the sword aside, the man then gave Ross a cloth that was the color of a pumpkin, somewhere between orange and gold. It measured about 8 inches square and had some Vietnamese writing on it. After showing Ross the writing by holding the cloth up by the corners, the man then folded it up until it was small enough to fit in the palm of his hand. Then he handed it to Ross, bowing his head as he did so. All the while, Genevieve had been telling Ross what the guy was saying. Her soothing voice helped calm his nerves. He was just happy when the ceremony was finally over. Genevieve put the cloth in her shoulderbag for safe-keeping.

Genevieve thought that since she and Ross were going to become husband and wife, she wanted Buddha to protect him and watch over him whenever they were apart. It was a special blessing, usually bestowed upon a special loved one. They were told that, as far as the Buddhist monk knew, Ross was the the only American to receive such a blessing.

Ross and Genevieve both thanked him and left his temple with a generous donation.

"Remember, never show anyone that cloth," she reminded Ross as they rode in the taxi back to their hotel.

"What would happen if somebody looked at it?" he wondered out loud.

"It would be very bad luck. Very bad," she replied with all seriousness.

CHAPTER 23

By the summer of 1972, U.S. ground forces had ceased all major operations in South Vietnam. There were only a few American combat troops left in the country by then, having handed over their responsibilities to their Vietnamese counterparts. There were fewer than 4,000 U.S. advisors now serving with ARVN units throughout the country.

The 1st Battalion, 7th Cavalry and the 3rd Battalion, 21st Infantry were the last U.S. infantry battalions to leave South Vietnam. At the U.S. president's direction, Vietnamization was in full swing.

The remaining bases that were still operating with U.S. aircraft assigned or attached temporarily like the A-4 Skyhawks of the Marine Corps at Bien Hoa, were protected mostly by Air Force security police forces and their USAF augmentees. Some of those augmentees performed guard duty at night and helped string more barbed wire, no longer able to rely on Army or Marine ground combat forces to help defend their bases. Usually, the Vietnamese guarded their portion of the base perimeter and Americans guarded their own.

    With no large American ground units conducting sweeps of areas to search out the enemy like in years past and South Vietnamese forces concentrating their forces around large cities and military bases, huge tracts of land lay open and unprotected. Large NVA forces were able to move around much more freely now than before. Their current offensive was causing havoc over a large area of South Vietnam. Casualties were high on both sides.
    Civilian airlines that contracted with the Department of Defense to transport American troops to and from South Vietnam through Bien Hoa Air Base, ceased operations there. Several aircraft had been damaged in the air by ground fire from around Bien Hoa and they deemed it too dangerous to fly in and out of that base any longer.
    Those were the conditions that existed when 1 Lt. Tom Ross drove there on July 31st. He had an uneventful trip for the most part. It became more intimidating when a gate guard at Long Binh gave him a warning about the dangers that lay ahead.
    He told Ross that some Army vehicles had been shot at recently on one of the roads between Long Binh and Bien Hoa. Because of that, some armored personnel carriers with .50 caliber machine guns mounted on top and a truck with quad .50s on it had taken up positions at a crossroads half-way between Long Binh and Bien Hoa.
    Playing it safe, Ross waited a few minutes just inside the base gate until a deuce-and-a-half drove up. There were two enlisted U.S. Marines inside the cab and two Air Force enlisted men sitting in the uncovered back on the side-facing bench seats. Ross told the driver he'd follow them to Bien Hoa, feeling safer driving behind the larger truck. There

was safety in numbers in this instance, he felt.

As the two military vehicles approached the outskirts of Bien Hoa City, the big 2½ ton truck in front slowed down. The Marine on the passenger side of the cab got out and stood on the running board. His left hand gripped the inside of the door and he put the stock of the 12-guage pump shotgun he'd been carrying, up against his right hip. He held it up in such a way that he could point the barrel towards any target that might suddenly appear in any open window they passed by.

When the truck drove past any two or three-story buildings, the Marine "riding shotgun" pointed the deadly weapon at every window while his eyes searched for a target. Grenades had been tossed from open windows down on military vehicles in the past. This vigilant Marine was determined to not let that happen today.

They arrived without incident and Ross checked in with OSI Detachment 5005's commander. Then he called his own unit back in Saigon to let them know he'd made it OK. The remaining three men of the detachment were almost done filling the four gray metal filing cabinets with their investigative paperwork. Ross was told they'd be ready with a forklift early the next morning to load up his truck.

He got directions to the Visiting Officer's Quarters (VOQ) and drove straight there. He was dirty, sweaty and tired and just wanted to take a relaxing shower and hit the sack early.

He asked the airman behind the check-in desk to give him a wake-up call at 0600. That would give him enough time to grab some chow, load up the cargo and get behind the big green Army shuttle bus at 0800 as it left Bien Hoa for Long Binh. He knew it stopped at USARV HQ there before continuing on to MACV HQ in Saigon.

Early the next morning Ross got a wake-up call of a different sort. It was around 0515 when all hell broke loose. He was literally blown out of his metal-framed GI bed. The concussion from a six-foot-tall, 122mm Russian-made rocket that exploded right across the street from the VOQ, sent him sprawling to the floor in a heap. The tremendous noise from the explosion and the painful landing his body made on the rock-hard linoleum-on-cement floor, jarred him instantly awake.

He landed on his right side and his hip and elbow both hurt like the devil. He struggled to put his uniform on as he lay on the floor. His plan was to take cover under the bed. "Hurry up! Hurry up!", his brain screamed.

There was a lot of noise from the multiple explosions, some really close, others far away, hitting randomly all across the base. It just continued on and on and the longer it did, the more nervous Ross got. It was the first time in his life he'd ever come under fire like this and it wasn't fun.

Once he thought he heard someone yelling but he couldn't understand what they were saying.

The base siren had gone off shortly after the first explosion. Now the noise from it joined in with the other noises and it sounded just like the tornado sirens he'd heard every spring back home in Oklahoma.

He finally got his uniform on and crawled under the bed, the only cover there was. Leaning against the outer walls of the building were big slabs of concrete. They were about six inches thick and four feet high. He'd noticed them when he checked into his room the day before and was somewhat comforted by the protection they provided from flying shrapnel. What worried him though was the thin tin roof and plywood ceiling overhead. Any mortars or rockets that dropped into his room from above would surely kill him and the bed offered little in the way of protection from a direct hit. Still, he thought, it was better than nothing.

The explosions continued after the siren stopped because it had taken a direct hit. Ross was worried that this might be an attack meant to overrun the base like the big attack during the 1968 Tet Offensive. He'd heard all about that one.

He wasn't a very religious person but today he prayed.

"Please God, make it stop." And just in case there was something to what Genevieve had told him, added, "Please Buddha, make it stop."

It seemed like the explosions had been going on for 15 to 20 minutes. It seemed like an eternity, especially when a few near misses shook the whole building. Ross could feel the close ones in every bone in his body. When the building shook, his whole body shook with it.

When the attack was finally over and he felt it was safe to go outside, he went to the office to check out. The airman behind the front desk was now wearing a helmet and flack jacket. Should have brought mine, he thought.

"Do you guys get attacked like this very often?"

"Not this bad, sir. Sometimes once or twice a month we'll get hit with three or four rockets but nothing as bad as this and I've been here almost a year. I think they hit us with a few dozen rockets and some mortars this time. Well, at least Command Post didn't call."

"What would that mean if they did?" Ross asked out of curiosity.

"That there's a ground attack and for everyone to get their weapons from the armory."

"Yeah," Ross responded to that bit of info,

"I'm glad they didn't call too."

He drove over to the main chow hall and got some biscuits and coffee. He was in a hurry to get his truck loaded up and hit the road. He'd had enough of Bien Hoa. Saigon seemed a whole lot safer and he was eager to get back. But, he had one more stop to make.

He wasn't bleeding anywhere but his elbow and hip hurt like the devil. He swung by the 6251st Combat Support Squadron's dispensary on the way to the OSI office. He wanted to have a doctor take a look, maybe get an X-ray and see if he'd broken anything.

When he got there, several people were standing off to one side of the building. It appeared to be heavily damaged, with the wall on the left side of the structure having been blown out. Parts of the wall and other debris were all over the ground. Some people were busy picking up pieces of it while others just stood there checking out the damage.

He was advised to seek medical treatment over at the 1st Cav side of the base if he wasn't hurt too badly. Everyone needing more than just a bandaid was being sent by helicopter to either Long Binh or Saigon. For the time being, this dispensary was out of action.

Ross thought he could still drive himself back to Saigon so he slowly and painfully got into his truck and drove to the OSI building. He hoped it hadn't been destroyed too.

The home of OSI Detachment 5005 was still intact. The file cabinets were loaded onto his truck with a small yellow 4K forklift and he delivered them to OSI Detachment 5006 at Tan Son Nhut later that day without incident.

Having completed his mission, he went over to the 377th USAF Dispensary ER and had his elbow and hip X-rayed. He was still hurting pretty bad and by now had two large bruises as evidence of his injuries. Nothing was broken and he was certainly glad of that. He left there with a medical duty excuse for the next day and a bottle of aspirin.

Ross knew how lucky he was to have come away from the attack on Bien Hoa with only some bumps and bruises. A few days later during a briefing at the 1st SIU, he learned that two American servicemen had been killed and fifteen wounded, not including him. The South Vietnamese military suffered seventeen wounded. In nearby Bien Hoa City, twenty civilians had been killed and a dozen more were wounded.

That evening he told Genevieve about the attack at Bien Hoa and how he'd gotten his bad bruises.

She saw this as an opportunity to convince him about some of her beliefs. Some people just needed more proof, like her father and Ross.

"You see? That is proof the Buddhist good luck ceremony really worked. Buddha protected you from death. Do you believe me now?" she asked, happy that he had not been injured too severely and equally happy for evidence of the good luck ceremony that protected him from certain death.

"Well, I guess I can't argue with that. I definitely was lucky," he admitted.

But that was all that he admitted to. There were still some things about some of her beliefs that he was just a little skeptical about. He did indeed feel very lucky. Lucky to have survived his first frightening time under fire and even luckier still to have found her. Just lucky, he thought. Nothing more than pure and simple luck.

That was all about to change.

It was around 7 p.m. on his very first night back. He was reading over the two-page list of items that they had to come up with in order to get married. She was watching a Vietnamese TV show, even though the screen was full of lines and the picture kept flipping every once in awhile. To Ross, it looked something like a Chinese play, performed on a stage in front of a live audience.

He was sitting on one side of the bed, she on the other, close to the street-side window and balcony.

He had provided his lawyer with a copy of the list and he was just reviewing it to make sure he didn't forget something. There were so many requirements, paperwork for both governments, interviews to go to, physical exams to get, background checks to be done, the list went on and on. One missed item might cause a delay and he didn't want that to happen.

Over the sounds of gongs, cymbols and singing coming from the TV, they both heard a commotion coming from the street directly below their second-floor room in the Federal Hotel. Ross watched as Genevieve jumped up and peeked out of the balcony door. She saw the police jeep and some men getting out of it. The officer in charge had already made his way to the front desk in the lobby and it was his loud, commanding voice they heard as he ordered his men to begin searching the building.

She quickly closed the door and turned off the old black and white TV set.

She pointed across the room at the other door.

"Make sure the door is locked and turn off the light. We must hide in the bathroom and not make a sound. Di di, di di!" she said excitedly.

Ross noticed that whenever she became alarmed and excited recently, she mixed words of different languages together, some bits of

French or bits of Vietnamese mixed with English. He didn't notice it until after they moved here. He understood that di di, when used this way in Vietnamese meant "go, go quickly." He was a fast learner.

"Another shakedown, looking for deserters?" he asked Genevieve in a whisper.

"Yes, I think so. Quiet now, let me listen." She never hesitated to take charge.

She put an ear to the door. Only a few rooms were presently occupied and the police made a quick search of those that were. She could hear demands for identification papers and for money. Nobody knocked on their door.

The extra money she'd given to the owner to keep quiet and not let anyone know about her and Ross had paid off. The owner told the police their room was unoccupied and they didn't want to waste any time with empty rooms. They had many buildings to check and the more they did, the more money their shakedown racket would produce. TO PROTECT AND SERVE was not one of the things stenciled on the sides of their vehicles.

As soon as the voices drifted back out to the street, Ross and Genevieve slipped quietly out of the bathroom. She cracked open the door to the balcony so she could hear what was being said down below.

She couldn't hear everything but what she did hear sent a chill through her. She heard Mang Binh Hao's name mentioned and that he'd be upset after paying them to find the whereabouts of the half-French, half-Vietnamese daughter of his French manager and they could not find her. Locating her would result in a big bonus. Therefore, they would continue with their search. Looking for military deserters was only a ruse. They were looking for her and a way to make some easy money even if she wasn't found. They drove off to look some more.

"We have to move again," she told Ross.

"Why? We've only been here for a couple of weeks. I thought you liked it here, so quiet and safe."

"I heard some of what the police said after they went back outside. Mang Binh Hao is paying a bonus to the police if they find where I live. If they come here again, the owner of this hotel might be persuaded to tell them about us. It is only because I gave him some extra money with the rent that he stayed quiet this time. I cannot trust him to stay quiet forever. We must go tomorrow."

With that said, she went over to where Ross stood and put her head on his chest, her arms around his back and gave him a hug.

"I am sorry I got you involved in this," she said as she began to sob.

"Nothing to be sorry about. We're in this together. Don't worry, you'll be safe with me, I promise," he said as he bent over and wiped a tear from her face and kissed her.

Then it dawned on him. "But I have to go on base tomorrow to do some more marriage paperwork. How will I be able to find you if you find another place?"

He was feeling really concerned about this on-going situation, and getting a little bit frustrated too. What the hell did Mang Binh Hao plan to do if he did find out where she was living? She doesn't know, her father doesn't know, somebody had to know! The only thing Ross could imagine was that Henri's old boss suspected that Henri had something he could use against him but surely he knew nothing about the journals. Right?

"Meet me at my father's house tomorrow night at 7. From there I will take you to a new place."

Neither one of them slept well that night.

They were both tense from the close-call of another police search and nervous about the slow progress of their marriage paperwork. Genevieve was worried about her father's deteriorating health and their safety as well. The aspirin Ross had taken helped him some but his elbow and hip were still both sore.

With so much going on in their lives, it seemed to be more than just a race against time. Time was running out for Henri as far as his cancerous brain tumor was concerned. Time was running out for Ross to get married, his current tour of duty too. Time was running out for Genevieve to find another place to live and stay safe. No wonder they didn't sleep well. Time was running out.

CHAPTER 24

Captain Daniels was about to address the gathering of officers of the 1st Special Investigations Unit. For a change, everyone was in uniform on this rainy day, except for the three CIA agents. A tropical deluge had soaked everyone on their way into the MACV compound that morning so things started out badly but then got much better for a change. At least for most people.

"You all knew this day would come, sooner or later," he began. "I've got your new assignment orders so it's PCS time again."

A few moans and groans from the small crowd.

"As I call out your name, come on up and get your orders and out-processing forms. After that, you're free to go. Make sure you get initials for all those places on the checklist that you're required to go to and don't miss any appointments. As of today, you're all released from regular duty. Just keep me posted if you're still working an active case so we can let the higher-ups know what's going on. Any questions?"

Someone asked, "Where are you going, Captain?"

"I'm getting out of the Army as soon as I get back to California. My brother-in-law invited me to join his firm as a private investigator in Los Angeles. Lots of work for PI's there and the pay is pretty good," he told the group, with a positive note of satisfaction in his voice. "Any other questions?"

There were none.

Maybe the rain had dampened their spirits as well as their uniforms, he thought. Nervous anticipation always seemed to accompany new assignments.

Looking at the orders in his hands, Daniels called out the first name.

"Bob Kosinski. Norfolk, Virginia. Come and get your paperwork."

He handed Kosinski his orders and out-processing form and then called out the next name.

"Daniel Ventnor. Annapolis, Maryland. Looks like your instructor duty request was approved."

The look of worry disappeared in an instant from Ventnor's face. Daniels took a sip of coffee after handing over the orders Ventnor had been hoping for. He was a very happy man now. Soaking wet, but all smiles.

"Jim Mahoney. Fort Lee, Virginia. Good assignment. I've been there. Wouldn't mind going back either."

The handing over of paperwork and calling out of names continued.

"Bill Fisher. Tyndall Air Force Base, Florida. Oh, poor guy! What's a young single man like you going to do in Panama City Beach?" he joked mockingly.

Some guys have all the luck when it comes to getting good assignments, Daniels mused.

"John Brenner, Steven Mann and Cecil Decker. Since you guys are obviously not GI's, your new posting was handled a bit differently. I've made each of you a copy of the message that came from your headquarters in Langley, Virginia that has your new assignment. You'll all be reporting to the Defense Attache Office in the American Embassy in Bankok, Thailand. I don't know what it's like to work there, but it's a hell of a nice place to take an R & R," he said with a mischievous grin.

His comment provoked a few laughs from those who knew what he was referring to.

"Joe Wagner. Pensacola, Florida. Another lucky guy that's going to be spending time on a white sandy beach!" he commented.

Several others still in the room agreed with him.

"Larry Johnson. Fort Huachuca, Arizona. Holy cow, who'd you piss off to get stuck way out in the desert like that?" Daniels jokingly asked.

"Actually, it's just what I wanted," came the reply. "I'm originally from Tucson and it's only about an hour drive from there," Johnson said, matter-of-factly. "At least it's a dry heat there, not like here," he said.

His boots made wet squishing sounds when he walked up to Daniels for his paperwork.

Good point, Johnson!

"Barry Westbrook. Travis Air Force Base, California."

Westbrook appeared to be satisfied as he came forward to get his orders.

Ross had been sitting patiently, wondering about where his next assignment might be. All this waiting for his name to be called was beginning to make him a little bit antsy with anticipation. All the other guys seemed to have gotten decent assignments. He hoped he would too.

"Tom Ross. Clark Air Base, Philippines,"

Daniels announced to a half-empty room.

A few other officers were milling around talking to others in hopes of learning something about their new assignments.

After getting his orders and out-processing form from Daniels, Ross decided to stick around too and see if anyone could tell him something about his new assignment.

One of the guys told him that he'd heard there had been some American GI's shot and killed in the town near the base and that their president had declared martial law. Another one suggested he take a helmet and flack jacket with him because of the anti-American activities over there.

Oh great, I'm leaving the fire for the frying pan, he thought. And I'm supposed to be taking Genevieve to a safer place. I'll just have to deal with it when we get there and hope we can get into base housing real quick. The last thing he needed now was more bad news.

Ross left the MACV compound, crossed the road and caught a Lambretta 3-wheeled taxi just inside the gate at Tan Son Nhut. For the equivalent of 15¢ in piasters, you could take a taxi ride anywhere on base. He had a lot of places to go before the day was through.

He was already familiar with CBPO, the Consolidated Base Personnel Office, because of the marriage paperwork he'd gotten from there. He also had to visit TMO, the Transportation Management Office, the Legal Office, Post Office, Accountiing and Finance too, just to name a few.

Somehow he had to find the time to write a letter to his parents and tell them he wouldn't be coming home any time soon. Unfortunately, they'd be meeting their new daughter-in-law at a much later date than they had anticipated.

Between all the out-processing paperwork and marriage paperwork, even with the help of a lawyer, he was going to be a very busy man over the next few weeks.

He pulled up at Henri's house in a familiar yellow and blue taxi. It was 6:55 p.m. Ross was still in his khaki 1505 uniform and still damp from the early morning soaking. The low clouds threatened to soak him again. Mai answered the knock at the door and let him in.

He found Genevieve kneeling down in front of her father, her head in his lap. Henri was sitting in his wheelchair, stroking her long dark hair and speaking to her in French in a low, calming voice. The only words Ross recognized and understood were "au contraire," on the contrary. Genevieve had been teaching him some French and Vietnamese words and phrases. He was a fast learner.

So much had changed since the last time he'd seen Henri. Ross was stunned by what he saw and apparently Genevieve had been too. Henri now looked much worse than before, looking older and thinner. Gaunt was the word that popped into his mind just then.

Henri could barely move his arms and then only with much difficulty. His words were being sounded out slowly because he was having a hard time speaking at a normal pace and at a normal volume.

Miss Lee, his live-in nurse, had to feed him because he kept dropping his fork. His food was now cooked and then put in a blender and turned into a baby food-like consistancy. Henri was having problems with chewing and swallowing regular food so the use of the blender had become necessary.

Miss Lee also had to help him in the bathroom. She had to bathe him and help get him on and off the toilet as well. It was pitiful how much his cancerous brain tumor had changed him, from a man who did everything for himself to a person who now required assistance with even the most basic things we all take for granted.

For a man in that poor condition, his mind was still sharp. In a low voice, which was all he had left, Henri asked Ross to wheel him into the kitchen for a cup of coffee and a private conversation.

Genevieve wiped her moist eyes dry and took a seat on the couch next to Miss Lee. Mai headed into the kitchen to prepare some coffee for the men and make some tea for the women. Once she left them alone with cups of fresh hot coffee, Henri began asking questions.

"How much longer before you and Genevieve can get married?"

His words came out slowly and with a degree of difficulty.

"I hope it won't be much longer. I've completed most of the paperwork, we've gotten our physical exams, we've been to the required counseling sessions. The lawyer I hired told me I had to go to the American Embassy myself to get my government's final approval once he gets the paperwork back from the Vietnamese police and gives it to me. I think that's about all there is other than go to the courthouse in downtown Saigon and post the bans of marriage. Once that's done, there's a ten-day waiting period before we can get married. Then after that, we can apply for her passport and visa."

Henri nodded in response then asked, "What is needed from the police?"

"A Certificate of Good Conduct. I think that's what the lawyer called it. It's to prove Genevieve has no police record."

Henri said, "Do not be surprised if that is delayed. Some of the police are paid by Hao. They may demand more money. They are capable de tout," he said, partly in English and partly in French. "Unpredictable, capable of anything, just like Mang Binh Hao," he said, with much disgust in his tone. "You get the visa from the American Embassy, no?"

"No, Henri. I just received my new assignment today. We'll be going to Clark Air Base in the Philippines from here, not to the U.S. Genevieve will get a Vietnamese passport, then we'll take it to the Philippine Embassy here in Saigon for a visa."

Henri didn't like hearing that but said nothing. He wanted his daughter to be as far away from Hao as possible, preferably in the United States. He thought she'd be much safer there. Hao or his henchmen could fly from Saigon to Manila in only two hours.

He reached into a pocket and slowly brought out a small silver key, almost dropping it before he could put it on the table. It was a struggle for him to get his arm to move even that much. As it was, he had to use both hands just to raise his coffee cup a few inches. He leaned far over to sip from it.

For Ross, it was such a pitiful sight and he felt so sorry for him. He wished there was something he could do for the man that may not live long enough to become his father-in-law.

"Put this in a safe place," Henri began. "There are three more journals locked in a small safe in my bedroom closet under some blankets on the floor. I know I do not have much longer to live." Almost as if he was reading his mind, Ross heard him add, "And I may not make it to your wedding to become your father-in-law either. You will marry my daughter regardless and take her away from here and make her happy. I know you will do that. You have a good heart. She has told me that several times. So, I will keep my part of the deal by giving you this key now before someone else finds it. I trust you to do the right thing."

He smiled at Ross and nodded his head approvingly. Ross was touched by his humbleness, sincerity and trust in him.

"Thank you, Henri. You can count on me. What will eventually happen to the people in those journals is out of my control but the safety of Genevieve is not. I want you to know that I will protect her with my life," he solemnly vowed. He meant every word too. "And there is something else you should know, Henri. I love Genevieve with all my heart and soul. I would have asked her to marry me anyway, even if you didn't give me the journals. Don't worry, I'll do the right thing," he concluded.

Ross felt better now that he'd gotten that off his chest. He wanted Henri to understand that he wasn't marrying his daughter just so he could have those journals. At the same time, he understood why Henri had approached him with the idea in the first place. He knew Henri would do **anything** to protect Genevieve.

"Merci beau coup, mon ami," Henri replied.

A tear slowly made its way down Henri's cheek. His wife would have been so proud of him. Now he would die a happy man. He felt so relieved that Genevieve would be in good hands and not left alone here after he was gone.

The engaged couple said their goodbyes that evening and headed across town to their new location. It started raining again but only a light drizzle. Genevieve told the taxi driver to drop them off at a street corner in Cholon, a couple of blocks away from the place she'd found for them. If anyone asked the driver, he wouldn't be able to give them their address.

They walked quickly down a narrow side street, trying not only to get out of the rain but to get out of sight too. The place she'd rented was a small, two-room, two-story wooden

THE SAGE OF SAIGON

building with a corregated tin roof, a typical Vietnamese house for this part of town. In 1968, the original building on this site had been destroyed during the heavy fighting between the Viet Cong and South Vietnamese forces during the Tet Offensive.

    The owner of the original building could not afford to replace it with one just like it so he opted for a much cheaper replacement. He then tried to sell the new building as a single-family home but priced it too high. After it stayed empty for awhile, he finally decided to rent it out. Even the amount he asked for as rent was beyond what the average Vietnamese could afford. Inflation was making prices on almost everything go up across the whole country at this time.

    Genevieve looked all over the city for a new place to live and was running out of options. She bartered with the owner until he finally lowered his asking price to something more reasonable. She had lots of experience bartering for lower prices. Every time she shopped for food in a local market she bartered for lower prices whether it was for rice, fish or vegetables. For her, bartering was a way of life and she was good at it too. She almost always got a better deal than the advertised price.

    The walls of the building were plain, unpainted wood both inside and out. She only had enough money to furnish it with the bare necessities. The bed was typical of rural Vietnam, a wooden plank bed with no mattress. A woven mat was spread across the planks to prevent splinters. Beds like this were used in other Asian countries too, including the Philippines.

    She had brought along their small oscillating fan from their first apartment. She had to buy a plain wooden wardrobe for her clothes and a hutch for odds and ends, including some clothing items that were normally folded up.

There were eight wooden steps built against the back wall that led up to the other room upstairs. Ross followed Genevieve as she showed him the rest of the place. She told him that because the upstairs room got so hot in the afternoons, she only planned on using it to hang up laundry to dry and to store things. The room was presently bare.

The only window in the ground floor room was a small one near the door. Other buildings were only inches away from both side walls and the back. She'd already covered the window with a curtain for privacy.

Back downstairs again, Ross stood there and looked around at the small place they'd be living in. It looked more like a shack than anything else, at least to him. Something was missing. He asked Genevieve where the bathroom was.

"There is no bathroom. There is a community toilet a few doors down from here but it stinks very bad, very dirty. We will use this bucket," she said, pointing to a red plastic bucket on the floor just under the edge of the bed. "I will empty it each morning in the community toilet."

Oh my God, he thought. "What about a shower?" Please let there be a shower.

"The big barrel outside the door catches rain water. We use that water in the washpan I bought and use a wash cloth and soap. All the people around us do that. It is only temporary. We will have a better place in the Philippines, right?"

He'd told her about his new assignment during the taxi ride over here. She didn't show any emotion about that one way or another. She didn't want him to know about the disappointment she felt by going there instead of the United States. She was looking forward to meeting his parents and seeing the place where he lived as a child. She was curious to see if there really were cowboys and Indians in Oklahoma or if Ross was just joking with her about that.

In any case, she was mentally prepared to go with him to wherever on earth the military sent him and make the best of it. At least, she thought, she'd be safer with him in the Philippines than here.

"Yes, we'll definitely get a better place there," he promised. "A whole lot better, I promise you. And what about food? Where will we eat?"

Ross had noticed the absense of a table or chairs.

"Many street vendors sell food near here. We will use the bed for a table so we do not eat on the floor. No problem, GI!" she said with a playful smile.

She could sense his disappointment in the place. That's why she tried to cheer him up with her own positive attitude, hoping it would make him feel better.

"Well, I'm missing that air conditioned hotel room already. It's hot in here," he complained.

"Xin loi mihn oi," she replied as she sat down on the wooden bed. "Lai day," she told him as she patted the spot next to her with her hand, looked up at him with her beautiful brown eyes and smiled.

He understood her when she said, "Sorry about that sweetheart," followed by, "Come here." He was a fast learner. And, he was fast in responding to the flirtacious invitation to sit next to her too, hard wooden bed or not.

"I have to tell you something," she said in a much-lowered voice. "If you hear any voices through the wall at night, just ignore it. It is only another GI and his girlfriend who are hiding out in the house next door."

"Why are they hiding out?"

"He ran away from the Army. If they find him, he will go to jail. There are many GIs hiding out in Saigon and Cholon so they can be with their girlfriends," she said.

"How do you know all this?"

"The girl next door told me when I came here the first time, so I would not be scared if I heard them talking or making noises at night."

"I hope you told her not to let anyone know about us living together."

"She will tell no one. She has a secret too."

Oh, that's just great, Ross thought. No air conditioning, no soft bed, no bathroom, no shower, and noises coming through the walls at night. All because some wealthy, big-time, mafia-style crook wants to harass my fiancee, to put the fear of God in her and her father so he doesn't spill the beans about illegal operations that she doesn't even know anything about. What in the world have I gotten myself into? Ross could only wonder what might happen next.

CHAPTER 25

Air power had provided the decisive edge the South Vietnamese needed to beat back the attacking forces of the NVA during the Easter Offensive. The enemy had underestimated the fighting resolve of the ARVN and South Vietnamese Marine units that chose to stand and fight. They also underestimated the resolve of the U.S. president to keep up the B-52 bombings and the resupply of tanks and artillery pieces the South Vietnamese forces lost in battle.

The NVA commander who failed to capture An Loc had a quick meeting with Nguyen Quoch Dinh before he retreated back across the border into neighboring Cambodia. The gist of the meeting between the general and the high-ranking Viet Cong member of the PRG, the Provisional Revolutionary Government was that this was only a temporary setback. Thanks to the U.S. news media, it was learned that the U.S. Congress was going to stop funding the war. At the Paris Peace Talks, American diplomats had stated that they were willing to stop fighting it as well. It was very convenient to have an adversary who announced their intentions ahead of time. As soon as the Americans were out of the war for good, NVA forces would return even stronger than before.

The PRG representative was directed to continue finding ways to undermine and weaken the Saigon government, its political and military leadership by any means possible. They were to begin identifying people who were their enemies as well. What happened to many civilians around the city of Hue during the Tet Offensive of 1968 may happen again. Thousands of people deemed enemies of the state there, were executed and buried in mass graves. A repeat of those actions was a distinct possibility.

Following that meeting, Dinh returned to Saigon to visit his friend, Mang Binh Hao. He knew that Hao had been playing both sides in the war in order to enrich himself. He warned him that he may end up on a list and Hao understood what he meant by that.

Hao heeded the warning and devised a plan to be out at sea on one of his cargo ships if things went bad. The longer the war lasted, the more money he stood to make. He already had a fortune stashed away in banks in different Asian countries. He owned some property in some of them too. He was a strong believer in that old saying, never put all your eggs in one basket.

Now it became important for him to make sure the timing of his departure from Saigon was just right. That was about the only thing he didn't have complete control over. Leaving too soon would cost him a small fortune in lost revenues. Leaving too late might cost him his life. Timing was everything.

The lawyer Ross had hired was finally able

to get the certificate of good conduct from the local police. Ross had been checking with the man every couple of days at his office in downtown Saigon. He'd been tempted to fire the man and not pay the other half of his fee.

They went over the list of things together just to make sure nothing had been overlooked. Ross felt it was necessary because he didn't totally trust the guy, especially after he asked for more money. He claimed he had to bribe the police to get some things done quickly. Quickly? To Ross, the whole process seemed to drag on forever. So over the checklist they went.

(1) Complete one copy of PACAF Form 80.
Check.

(2) Make four copies of that form for 7th Air Force.
Check.

(3) Birth certificates for both parties.
Check.

(4) Complete chronological record of each residence where intended spouse has lived since birth, utilizing MACV Form 448 EV and typed in English.
Check.

(5) Vietnamese police certificate of good conduct of the intended spouse covering entire period of residence in the Republic of Vietnam.
Check.

(6) Statement of non-previous marriage signed by the intended spouse using MACV Form 446 EV.
Check.

(7) Statement by the Personnel Officer (CBPO-DC) indicating that the applicant's records do not disclose evidence of a prior marriage.
Check.

(8) Statement of counseling of both parties by the Chaplin.
Check.

(9) Sworn statement of your ability to support your intended spouse. Letter format obtained from the Legal Office.
Check.

(10) Detailed statement of assets obtained from the military pay section of Personnel.
Check.

(11) Statement of Cola and Travel, Statement of Visa, Statement of Ramifications, Statement of Withheld Privileges and Statement of Departure of intended spouse.
Check. Check. Check. Check. And check.

(12) Report of physical exam of both parties by the U.S. Medical Corps Officer, recorded on Form FS-398 (Medical Examination of Visa Application).
Check.

Ross had to take Genevieve to the 17th U.S. Army Field Hospital at 263 Tran Hung Dao in Saigon for her exam. It cost him $7.00 and a round-trip taxi fare, but to him, it was worth every penny.

(13) Six copies of MACV Form 429-R (Biographic Data) of your intended spouse, witnessed by a commissioned or warrant officer and typed in English.
Check.

(14) Statement of counseling by the Legal Officer.
Check.

After being satisfied that all the required paperwork to get married in Vietnam was completed, Ross gave the lawyer the other half of his fee. He had doubts as to whether or not his money had been well spent. It just didn't seem like the lawyer got things done quicker than he could have by doing it all himself. Only time would tell.

Nonetheless, Ross let out a long sigh of relief. He thought this day would never get here. Just two more places to take the pile of paperwork, the American embassy over on Thong Nhut Boulevard and then over to Cach Mang Boulevard, a main thoroughfare that goes to downtown Saigon where the main courthouse is. He'd have to take Genevieve with him to the courthouse. His Vietnamese still wasn't good enough to explain what he needed there or to understand their instructions to him.

It was a good thing he'd brought Genevieve along when he turned in the paperwork at the courthouse. The man he handed it to went on and on as if he was giving a speech or something. The guy typed up a form, put some kind of documentary stamp on it and asked for some money to pay for it. Then he got up from his paper-covered desk and stapled that same form onto a cork board that was on a wall out in the hall just outside of his office.
Now it was official. The bans of marriage had been posted. The paper would stay up on that board for ten days, announcing to the general public the intended marriage between Tom Ross and Genevieve Ferrand. If nobody contested it, they'd be able to get married. If it was contested, well, things could get a little complicated. Really complicated, the man in the courthouse told them.
Because they didn't have much time left before Ross had to leave for the Philippines, they planned on a simple non-denominational ceremony in the American embassy chapel. After the wedding, they'd rush over to the Philippine embassy and get a visa for her Vietnamese passport so she could travel with her American husband. Nothing like a little

international diplomacy.

Ross would have to get his travel orders changed from unaccompanied status to accompanied and have her name put on them as well. She would also have to be added on his MTA in order to travel on the same plane. There was still so much to do and so little time left to do it all.

Meanwhile, Henri had Mai go into town and send a telegram to his brother in France. He wanted his younger brother, Pierre, to fly to Saigon so he could see him one last time.

Pierre Ferrand was the only family he had left in France. Henri also wanted him to see Genevieve since he hadn't seen her in a very long time, eighteen years to be exact. He could also help her through the hard times ahead. It would be nice for Pierre to meet Ross as well.

Unfortunately, by the time Pierre arrived after traveling half-way around the world on an Air France 747 jumbo jet, Henri had taken his last breath. Just a few hours before his plane landed, Miss Lee had to take him to the French-run Grall Hospital because he was having difficulty breathing. By that time, Henri was unable to do anything for himself at all. His nervous system had almost completely shut down and only his heart was still able to move on its own. He had a very strong heart, the heart of a lion.

When he was brought into the ICU, Intensive Care Unit, his eyes were closed and his breathing was very labored and noisy. He struggled mentally to live on as long as possible, hoping to find that his beloved enfant cheri had become Mrs. Tom Ross. Then he knew she would be safe and he would die a happy man.

His private nurse sent Mai to get Genevieve in Cholon but when she arrived there nobody was home. She left a message with one of the neighbors and it was several hours before Genevieve got it from the young woman who was hiding her GI boyfriend.

By the time she arrived at the ICU, her father was already gone, as in, no longer physically there. They had taken him to another part of the hospital where the deceased remained to be viewed and claimed by family members. Miss Lee took her to him.

Pierre Ferrand was later escorted to that room by a member of the hospital staff. There, standing over his older brother Henri, he saw his niece for the first time in a very long time. She had been there for a couple of hours already. When she turned to see who had moved next to her, he could see how red her eyes and nose were from all the crying she'd done. While most women would look terrible in that condition, she was still an attractive young woman.

Henri's still form was laying on a gurney, covered up to his neck by a plain white sheet. His eyes were closed and his face was expressionless, pale and gaunt. Though he was only 56 years old, Pierre thought he looked much older than that. In fact, he barely even recognized him. The last time he'd seen him in person was in 1954 when he'd visited Henri, his wife and their 2-year-old daughter when they still lived in the coastal city of Vung Tau.

Pierre looked a little younger than his age of 53. He was also slightly taller and thinner than his older brother. They had the same dark brown hair and thick eyebrows. He bent over to kiss his brother's cheek in a final farewell.

"Dieu vous garde, Henri." God keep you.

Then he too broke down and started sobbing and the flow of tears began. Genevieve reached over and put an arm around him and gave him a consoling hug.

Mai and Miss Lee were standing over on the far side of the dimly lit room, giving the two family members some privacy in their time of grief. They too had already shed some tears for the man who'd treated them both with respect and kindness. They would miss him a lot. They had never known a man like this Frenchman before and doubted they ever would again.

For the second time in her young life, 20-year-old Genevieve felt a big void in her life. First her mother had died when she was only 11 and now her father was gone too. A piece of her died with them. Now with her father gone too, life would never be the same.

At least she had Ross in her life so she wouldn't be left all alone. She hated to think what her life would be like now with both parents dead if she didn't have Ross. It was fate. It was meant to be, she thought.

Her Uncle Pierre would only be here until her father was buried. He would have to return to France, to his family, his home and his job. Then it would be just her and Ross, at least until they decided to start a family. They really had not talked about that yet. There would be plenty of time to talk about that later.

When Ross finished his business on base, he went to their new "hide-out" as he called their new place in Cholon. He waited around inside for awhile but when Genevieve didn't show up by late in the afternoon, he sensed something was wrong. She had left him no note and she'd never been away from home this late in the day.

He changed out of his uniform and into his civvies and then took a taxi to Henri's house, arriving there after it was already dark out. It seemed like every light was on in the house and he'd never seen that before during any of his previous visits. That seemed mighty strange. Plus, there were a few cars parked at the curb. That wasn't normal either, especially not ones with drivers and armed guards standing next to a couple of them. Something out of the ordinary was going on for sure.

Mai met Ross at the door as usual, but who were all these people, he wondered, as Mai led him to Genevieve, surrounded by people he'd never seen before. And where was Henri?

Genevieve excused herself from her guests and went up to Ross, hugging him tightly. He could tell she'd been crying. Her eyes were very red and puffy and she looked tired, worn-out tired.

"What's going on, mihn oi?" he asked.

They'd gotten into the habit of calling eachother "sweetheart" in Vietnamese. Kind of like American couples who call eachother "honey."

"Who are all these people?"

Trying hard not to break down and cry again, she said, "My father died earlier today."

"Oh no. I'm so sorry." His brain went numb for a minute and that's all he could think to say. He hugged her tight and kissed the top of her forehead. Her face was pressed tight against his chest as they embraced.

She told him, "By the time I arrived at the hospital he was already dead. His younger brother Pierre flew all the way from France to see him before he died but he got there too late also."

"I'm so sorry, Genevieve. Mihn oi, I'm so sorry."

Even knowing in advance that Henri was dying didn't prepare Ross for the actual shock of his death. He'd been hoping it wouldn't happen even while he knew it eventually would. He felt numb. Henri was dead now. This is for real. His inner voice was telling him, you have to deal with it man, just deal with it. You've got to be strong for Genevieve. Snap out of it. She's depending on you. The inner voice in his mind rarely failed him when it came to advice on what to do.

"So, who are all these people?" he asked again.

First he was introduced to Henri's younger brother, Pierre Ferrand. He was taller than Ross, about 5'11" and slightly stockier too, weighing around 175 pounds, give or take. He could see the family resemblance between the brothers. Even Pierre's dark gray suit looked like one of Henri's.

Then he was introduced to a long-time friend of Henri's, Ngai Bien Phong, Minister of National Defense. He was the one with the driver and uniformed armed guards around his car. One of the other cars had armed guards in civilian clothes. He told Ross that he and Henri had met in Marseille, France many years ago. They were very good friends.

The next introduction made Ross a little bit uncomfortable to say the least. Mang Binh Hao, owner of Gulf of Lion Shipping Company and Henri's boss had also stopped by to pay his respects. He also wanted to find out about the funeral and burial arrangements. He offered his condolences to Genevieve, never revealing how he'd found out about Henri's death. She had not been the one who'd informed him.

Hao assumed that her American boyfriend would accompany her to the cemetary. The only man who knew more about what was going on around Saigon than Henri did was Hao. He took a few moments to share some of his thoughts about Henri with Ross. As he did so, he looked the American over closely, thinking that he looked out of place in his blue jeans, large metal belt buckle and Western boots. In the room full of mourners, he stuck out like a sore thumb.

Ross was then introduced to the Catholic priest who ran the school Genevieve had attended. Then he was introduced to a Buddhist monk before he was able to talk to Genevieve alone. The monk had been the spiritual advisor to both her and her mother.

She suggested they live in her father's house from now until they left the country together. She would get Mai to help her move their belongings from Cholon to here while he finished his out-processing, worked on their marriage paperwork and arrangements with the American embassy to use their chapel. She had to settle her father's affairs and could do it better from right here in his house. After all, everything he owned was here and it made perfect sense to Ross.

It made him feel good to hear her say these things, proving even more that he was going to marry a very intelligent young woman with a good head on her shoulders who could think for herself. She had other ideas too.

She would bury her father next to her mother in Vung Tau and her uncle would go with her to her mother's ancestral family cemetery. That would give Ross some time to work on passport and visa paperwork, get his orders changed and her name added to his MTA so she could accompany him on the flight from Tan Son Nhut to Clark Air Base. Again, it all made sense to him.

Those were the plans they discussed and agreed to. There was still so much they had to do and time was quickly running out. Ross had already received a port call, flying out of Tan Son Nhut on a Continental Airlines B-707. His blue MTA, Military Transportation Authorization was his ticket out of the country on a "freedom bird." According to his short-timer calendar, he was now a single-digit midget with only 9 days left in-country.

Reflecting back on his introduction to Mang Binh Hao, Ross was still wondering about Hao's reference to Henri being the sage of Saigon. Hao told him about the many business deals Henri had made that increased his company's profits for 25 consecutive years, an unheard of accomplishment in most businesses.

"A man with all the qualities of wisdom, prudence, good judgement and an in-depth knowledge of how things are done in this country is truely a sage by anyone's definition," he'd said to Ross.

He'd spoken with such a big smile on his face that one might think he was bragging about a son instead of an employee that worked under implied threats.

And all that information he wrote down in his journals is going to bite you and some others in the ass some day, Ross thought in response. Then he wondered if Henri's death might also mean that Hao would now have no reason to harass or threaten Genevieve in any way. After all, he'd only used threats as a scare tactic so Henri would keep quiet. Wouldn't Henri's death change all that? He wasn't sure about Hao's plans now so he and Genevieve would just try and keep a low profile and stay alert to be on the safe side. Nine more days from now and they'd never give Mang Binh Hao a second thought ever again.

Pierre Ferrand stood in for his brother and signed the paperwork as a witness to the marriage of his niece, Genevieve Ferrand to

Tom Ross. The simple ceremony was held in the small chapel of the American embassy. The beautiful young bride wore a new all-white au dai and the handsome young groom wore his all-blue Air Force dress uniform. They looked amazing together.

The chaplin conducted the non-denominational ceremony with the traditional finishing words, "I now pronounce you man and wife." Then he smiled at them and added, with a twinkle in his eyes, "You may now kiss the bride."

It was his favorite part of the ceremony as well as the bride and groom's. Pierre took a few pictures of the couple with his fairly-new instamatic camera. The chaplin took a couple of pictures of the three of them too. Pierre would take some more pictures during his trip to Vung Tau with his niece and then get the film developed after returning to Saigon.

As the smiling newlyweds left the chapel, a small gathering of embassy employees threw rice at them and cheered. These days there hadn't been much to cheer about. Then Ross, Genevieve and her Uncle Pierre left the embassy compound in a very happy mood.

Mai had helped Genevieve move their things into her father's house. There hadn't been much, especially after Genevieve sold the few pieces of furniture they had.

While Genevieve was with Ross and her uncle at the American embassy, Mai was busy removing some of their clothes that had been boxed up in Cholon. She knew Genevieve had a lot to do so she volunteered to stay behind and unpack the boxes for her.

As she lifted some of Genevieve's clothes

out of one of the cardboard boxes, a small folded cloth the color of a pumpkin, somewhere between orange and gold, fell to the floor. It had been placed on top of some white T-shirts when Genevieve packed the clothes. Then she'd placed some of her things on top of the special cloth.

At first Mai thought it was just a fancy handkerchief. When she bent down and picked it up by a corner, it unfolded to reveal some Vietnamese writing and some symbols on one side. Then she held it up by two corners and the whole thing was now open to view. Choi oi! She quickly realized what she'd seen and dropped it to the floor as if it had burned her fingers as a look of fear spread across her face.

Not knowing what else to do, she carefully folded it back up with shaking hands and much apprehension. She then stuck the cloth between a couple of layers of clothing that had already been placed on top of the dresser.

Of all the days for this to happen, on Genevieve's wedding day no less, she had accidently seen something that only two people on earth were allowed to view. Then she prayed to Buddha for forgiveness.

CHAPTER 26

Shortly after the wedding, Ross took his new bride on base to get her a military dependent ID card. Then after leaving the Pass & ID section they headed over to another part of CBPO to get his assignment orders changed from unaccompanied to accompanied status.
He was told to come back in two days and pick up the amendments to his orders. Once orders were cut, he was told, they weren't changed. A separate amendment to the orders would be prepared. He also had to get his MTA changed but that and a few other last-minute things would have to be done later. That was all they were able to get done that day.
Ross and Genevieve agreed that there wasn't enough time for a honeymoon and talked about maybe going on a trip to some nice beach somewhere in the Philippines. He could only imagine how hot she would look in a bikini on a nice sandy beach. Oh yeah. A honeymoon on the beach. He was looking forward to that already.
They discussed the next day's events too.

She and her uncle would be heading to Vung Tau with her father's casket. He would be buried next to her mother in her family's ancestral cemetery. She would light incense sticks and pray for both of their souls. Then she and her uncle would return the next day. It wasn't safe traveling any roads at night which was why no passenger busses did. The night belonged to Victor Charlie out in the countryside.

While she was away, Ross would be very busy trying to get all the last-minute things done, spending most of his time at Tan Son Nhut. He still had to turn in his key to the billeting office downtown and his weapon to the MACV armory so he could get those two things initialed on his out-processing checklist. Time was quickly running out and there was still much to do.

Genevieve rented a hearse to transport her father's coffin from Saigon to Vung Tau. She and Uncle Pierre would ride in it to the cemetery and then for the return trip, they'd ride in a regular passenger bus that made the round trip between the two cities on a regular basis.

As they stood in front of Henri's house that morning waiting for the hearse to show up, Ross told Genevieve, "Be careful, OK?"

She was standing next to him in her traditional ao di, he in his Western attire of blue jeans, large metal belt buckle and boots. The yin and yang of East and West.

"Do not worry. The road to Vung Tau is safe. There is no fighting anywhere between here and there. I will not be alone. My uncle will be with me all the time. Not to worry."

She smiled up at him and gave his hand a loving squeeze. She wasn't worried and he shouldn't be either, she felt.

"OK, I guess I worry too much," he admitted and returned her pretty smile with a smile of his own.

    The long black hearse, looking like its best days were back in the 1950s, finally showed up. There was a ton of chrome on the front and rear and it had large pointed fins on the rear quarter panels. The windows were all tinted very dark.

    For the very first time, Ross ignored the Vietnamese cultural norms (intentionally) about displays of public affection. He gave his beautiful young wife a goodbye hug and a long, lingering kiss. He didn't give a damn who might be watching.

    "I love you," he said, probably for the tenth time already that day.

    He never tired of telling her because he meant it and he hoped she would never tire of hearing it.

    She told him something in Vietnamese that sounded like, "Anh hieu em nhieu lam mai mai soot doi," meaning, I love you very much forever.

    At least that's how he interpreted it. He was still working on his translating skills, fast learner notwithstanding. It didn't matter to him if she spoke Vietnamese, English or French. Her voice had a magical quality to his ears and he loved to hear her talk, no matter what she said. Her voice had had the same effect on him the first day they met and it probably would forever.

    He waved goodbye as the old dark car slowly pulled away, not seeing her because of the darkly tinted glass. He had hoped to catch one last glimpse of her as he waved. The cops would have pulled him over if he tried that dark tint on his car back in Oklahoma, he thought.

    The trip along Highway 51 was a slow, yet

uneventful one for Genevieve and her Uncle Pierre. The 80-mile-long stretch of road between Saigon and Vung Tau was regularly patrolled by military vehicles and there were a few police checkpoints along the way. It made the travelers feel safe.

Pierre was surprised at how well his niece spoke French with the accent of one who was a native of Marseille, like he and his brother. They had a lot to talk about and the leisurely pace of the ride gave them the opportunity to learn about eachother. He had not seen her since she was two years old and much had changed with them both over the past 18 years.

Late that afternoon, just when it began to blend in with early evening, Henri Ferrand was laid to rest for all eternity next to his beloved wife, Nguyen Thi Kieu. Their deaths had occurred nine years apart.

Now they would be together again forever, Genevieve thought, as she knelt down and lit some incense. She prayed to God and Buddha for their souls. Pierre knelt down next to her and silently prayed as well.

They went into town as the sun began to set and shadows covered much of the surrounding landscape. They had supper in a hotel named Metro House, known for its French restaurant and Mediterranean villa-like looks. Pierre told Genevieve about his visit with her family when she was just a toddler. He told her what a coincidence this was to be eating here again after so many years. They all had supper here back in 1954 and to him, everything still looked the same.

Even the street sign had remained unchanged, showing this to be Tran Hung Dao Street. Many good memories flooded back nostalgically in his mind. He only wished his brother and sister-in-law were still with them now. Just thinking about those wonderful memories brought tears to his eyes.

"What is wrong, uncle?" she asked in French.

"I was just remembering my visit here when you were just a baby. Your moma and papa were still young and so happy then. And now... c'est la vie," that's life, he said. "I'm sorry. I'm supposed to be here to help you be strong, for my brother's sake, and look at me. I am the weak one. I'm sorry."

He wiped his eyes dry with the cloth napkin and tried to put on a brave face but he just couldn't do it. His heart was still crying out for his brother Henri. He didn't know his older brother's passing was going to be like this.

He reached out for Genevieve's hand and told her, "You're so lucky to have a husband now at a time like this. You must lean on his shoulders and find comfort in his arms. Your papa would want that, I'm sure. He wanted you to be happy, to have someone to love after he was gone. After I return home, you will not be alone. Take comfort in that," he said as he smiled at her and gave her hand a light squeeze.

"Thank you, uncle. Yes, I am very lucky to find a good man in this time of war and death. And when we get back to Saigon, I will tell him that he will be a father too and I know he will be a good one."

With a very surprised look on his face, he asked, "You're pregnant?"

"Yes. I just found out the other day. It was not the right time to tell Tom, what with Papa dying and so much to do this week. So yes, you will have another relative next year and I will become a mother. Imagine that! I cannot wait to see the look on his face when I tell him. He will be so happy too." Her face was glowing with joy as she said that.

While his wife was away in Vung Tau, Ross had trouble sleeping by himself in Saigon. He'd gotten used to cuddling with Genevieve every night. He missed that already. That, along with something else was bothering him and he couldn't stop thinking about it.

When he arrived at Henri's house as he still called it, Mai didn't answer his knocks at the door as she normally did. He had his own key now and after several more knocks went unanswered, he let himself in.

He searched every room, not only to look for Mai but to see if he could notice anything out of the ordinary, something out of place, maybe something missing.

Nothing. No Mai, everything appearing to be normal, at least until he finished thoroughly searching her room. All of her clothes and belongings were gone.

By the time he'd gone to bed he'd asked himself a lot of questions. Where did she go? Most importantly, why did she go? Had Genevieve told her we would be leaving the country soon and she could start looking for a new job? Those unanswered questions and the absense of Genevieve to snuggle up to, kept him from having a good night's sleep.

Pierre and Genevieve boarded a small passenger bus at the main bus depot in Vung Tau the next morning. They took a seat near the center, between the two axels. It was a less bumpy ride near the middle of the bus, Genevieve told her uncle. She'd taken bus rides between Vung Tau and Saigon at least once a year so she knew from experience where the best seats were. They were the only passengers on the bus that day wearing the dark clothing of mourners.

A young man watched them as they took their seats. Once he was certain that he'd identified the American man and pretty half-French, half-

Vietnamese woman and the bus they were on, he got on his motor scooter and headed out of town. He had no idea the man was her uncle. The long-nosed guy looked like an American to him.

    He was almost half-way to Saigon when he saw the flashing signal from a mirror, almost blinding him at times. He pulled off the road and gave the man the information he wanted about those two particular passengers and the bus they were on. He counted the piasters the man paid him, then got back on the road again, headed for Saigon. He didn't know just what the man was going to do with the information he gave him and he really didn't care. He had some more money in his pocket now. That's all he cared about.

    Looking through some high-power binoculars, the man in charge saw the passenger bus approaching his position along Highway 51. Traffic was fairly light right now with most vehicles anywhere from 75 to 100 yards apart. Then when they approached the occassional cart pulled by a water buffalo, they tended to bunch up a little as they slowed down and found a spot to pass. The road had many pot holes in it and was in need of repaving, so speeds were never very high on this stretch of the two-lane highway.

    It was late morning now, sunny, hot and humid. Shimmering heat waves could be seen across the asphalt road surface at a distance. Puffy white cumulus clouds were only now beginning to appear in the sky, casting large dark shadows on the ground here and there. Visibility was perfect all the way out to ten miles.

    As the bus drew nearer, the man with the binoculars leaned against the overturned ox cart out in an open field on the north side of the road and steadied his hand. He rotated the focus knob to zoom in on the passengers seated near the middle of the bus. He saw an attractive young woman near a window, definitely not 100% Vietnamese, even in an ao dai. He tried to see who was sitting next to her. Yes, that's definitely a big-nosed American for sure, he thought. They were sitting exactly where their informant had said. Too bad about the rest of the people on the bus.

There had been no rest for the 10-man VC squad out on Highway 51 that night. They were very skilled at their craft, even in the dark of night. They turned an unexploded 155mm artillery shell into a deadly land mine. They buried it just deep enough in the sandy soil so that nobody could see it, right at the edge of the road. When it was electrically detonated the same way a Claymore mine was, it was powerful enough to destroy any size or type of vehicle, even a tank, instantly killing all the occupants.

Their orders had come from Nguyen Quoch Dinh, a man much higher in rank in their organization than any of them. He told them that the two passengers they were keeping tabs on may have been given some information about several high-ranking military officers and government officials who were pro-VC. The information had been acquired from the woman's father, an employee of Mang Binh Hao. It was essential that this damaging information not get passed on to American and South Vietnamese officials who could then use it against the supporters of their cause.

The fact that anyone else traveling with the couple would be killed too was inconsequential to the VC. As they had learned while fighting the French 20 years ago, c'est la guerre. That's war; it can't be helped. The death of Henri Ferrand and his burial in Vung Tau had presented Hao and the VC the perfect

opportunity to tie up another loose end.
   When the bus arrived at the predetermined spot, the man with the binoculars gave the verbal orders and another man set off the huge mine. The deafening blast roared across miles of flat open ground. A dark mushroom cloud with a fiery red and yellow center shot high into the morning sky. The concussion wave rocked the cart next to the man with the binoculars, causing him and his partner-in-crime to tumble over backwards as they cringed and held fingers in their ears. The others in their unit were already long gone.
   The bus temporarily disappeared in the initial blinding flash of the powerful explosion. It was torn apart into many pieces, most of which flew high into the air before falling back to the ground, mostly on the south side of the road.
   The fuel tank had ripped open and flames appeared on almost every piece of metal, glass, rubber, plastic and human body part that lay scattered around for many yards. The spare tire had landed a quarter of a mile away, right next to a foot still wearing a Ho Chi Minh sandal.
   The driver and his 35 passengers, 36 if you count one fetus, died instantly. Four of the passengers had been young children under the age of ten. Many of the people were blown into pieces, a head here, a leg there, several half-torsos landing on the pavement or in the dirt off to one side of the road or the other. A couple of the bodies had been totally obliterated. It was a terribly gruesome sight.
   Some of the passengers were burned beyond recognition while those that weren't were no longer identifiable for various reasons. It was a horrific scene that greeted the first people that showed up to see if they could help save anyone. There was nobody left to

save.

Trying to identify the human remains of this tragic and bloody carnage was next to impossible. Most of the forms of ID carried by the passengers were either destroyed by fire or were blown away from the owners and heavily damaged.

When the ARVN military police unit assigned to patrol this area showed up, they dug a deep trench in the field on the north side of the road. That's where they buried all the body parts they found scattered all around. The unrecognizable badly burned skeletal remains were buried there too. In this war, mass graves like this one were not uncommon. It was a thankless job this unit had done a couple of times before.

The mangled steel frame of the bus had landed on its side and all the tires were burning off the rims. The roof and sides of it had been blown completely off the frame and lay around in many charred and mangled pieces.

Both lanes of traffic were blocked for a few hours. Some vehicles managed to drive around the carnage by cutting through the fields on either side, dodging the burning debris and burning dry grass.

Ross was really worried now. He hadn't heard from Genevieve and her uncle for two days. He went to the American embassy first, then the nearby French embassy, trying to get someone to help him find out what could have happened to his wife and her French uncle.

He went to the Vietnamese national police headquarters too, having to hire an interpreter to help him. He was growing more concerned with each passing hour. He even went to MACV headquarters to see if any military unit still left in the country could help him.

After running low on energy, he stopped in the snack bar on the ground floor of MACV HQ to grab a burger and some coffee to help him keep going. He hadn't slept a wink in 36 hours. Someone in the snack bar showed him a front page article in the Pacific Stars and Stripes newspaper.

A free-lance photographer had taken a picture of a terrible scene he'd come upon while traveling down Highway 51, half-way between Saigon and Vung Tau. The story beneath the black and white photo was about a passenger bus that had been blown up by a land mine planted by the Viet Cong. They estimated that between 35 and 40 people aboard that bus had perished in the explosion. The only thing recognizable in the photo was the charred, mangled steel frame and wheels of a vehicle. It was turned on its side and the tires were still burning with lots of black smoke billowing upwards.

A shiver ran down his spine as Ross read the horrible story. He prayed that Genevieve and her uncle hadn't been on that particular bus.

The following morning he was back at the MACV HQ snack bar again, this time for some breakfast. He'd only managed to doze off for a few minutes at a time that night and his nerves were shot. He looked like hell when he saw himself in the mirror that morning while shaving and he felt like it too. Still no word from Genevieve or her uncle. He told everyone he'd asked help from that this would be where he could be contacted in case someone had some news for him. His plane was due to leave in only two more days. Time was running out.

The U.S. Army and the CIA ran a Phoenix

Program advisor's school in Vung Tau. On average, 25 military intelligence officers attended the week-long class. It was closed now, a victim of the president's Vietnamization program. One of the officers who taught the last class held there was sent back to Vung Tau by the commanding general of MACV. Lieutenant General Albert Christianson had heard about the dilemma Ross was facing. Ross had turned over three more of Henri's journals to him, what the commander of MACV referred to as "the holy grail of intel," full of names, details of illegal activities, etc. It was understandable why the general felt compelled to help Ross out if he could.

For an entire day Ross nervously walked the halls of MACV HQ, frequenting the snack bar, waiting for some information, hopefully good, about Genevieve and her uncle. Her mysterious absence was driving him crazy. Why hadn't she returned yet? Could she possibly have been on the bus that had been blown up? Please God, don't let that be the case, he begged.

He went another night with hardly any sleep, only nodding off every now and then for a few minutes at a time. Even after a shower and shave, he still looked haggard and beat.

Morning came and his plane was due to leave at 1200, high noon. At 0900 the officer who'd gone to Vung Tau met with him in the snack bar where he'd been nervously waiting. He didn't want to get on that plane without the love of his life, Genevieve. He was optimistically hoping for some good news.

"What did you find out?" he asked as he stood up from the table.

Tired as he was, he focused on the guy's face and recognized that look right away. It was not the facial expression of one bearing good news. In fact, it caused him to unconsciously hold his breath in anticipation of the reply.

"Your wife and her uncle got on the same bus together in Vung Tau, one that was going to Saigon. That much I know for sure. But, their bus never made it. They were on the one that got blown up on Highway 51 a couple of days ago. I'm terribly sorry."

Ross didn't hear the last three words that were spoken to him. His face went blank and his eyes rolled back as he passed out and fell to the floor with a loud thud.

His scheduled flight to the Philippines took off without him and Genevieve. He ended up leaving Vietnam on a stretcher the next day as a patient aboard a C-9 Nightingale medical evacuation plane, along with several other American casualties of the war. He woke up several days later in a strange place. A doctor was shining a small flashlight in his eyes.

"Lieutenant Ross, can you hear me?"

Ross squeezed his eyelids together first, then slowly opened them. His eyes felt hot and dry.

He asked the doc, "Where am I?" He was totally disoriented and still in a mental fog.

"You're in the 13th Air Force Regional Medical Center at Clark Air Base in the Philippines," came the reply.

"What am I doing here? I've got to go look for Genevieve." She was the first thing that popped into his semi-conscious mind.

He tried to sit up but couldn't. He was strapped down to the bed. Even his wrists were bound to the railing on either side of him.

The doctor, an elderly full-bird colonel, asked him, "Who's Genevieve?"

"She's my wife. Can I go now? I've got to find her," he pleaded.

He still looked like he was disoriented and his heart rate was increasing as the doctor scanned the monitors Ross was hooked up to.

Ross was obviously confused, still thinking that Genevieve was still alive and he needed to find her before their plane took off from Tan Son Nhut. Being told where he was hadn't changed a thing. He thought he was still in Vietnam and he and Genevieve had a plane to catch.

The doctor checked the medical chart at the end of his bed and then gave him another shot. His breathing gradually slowed.

The last thing he heard before falling back into a deep sleep was Genevieve's soft voice, speaking in Vietnamese, her beautiful French-accented words that meant, "I love you very much forever."

EPILOGUE

The six journals that Henri Ferrand had compiled over the years while working for Mang Binh Hao, provided a treasure-trove of intel for both the American and South Vietnamese governments. The problem was, it was such an embarrassment to the Vietnamese that they decided to do what they'd been doing all along. They told the Americans what they wanted to hear instead of the truth.
They would look into the accusations and, if warranted, remove those who were found guilty from their commands or offices and see that they were punished.
No action was ever taken by South Vietnamese officials against anyone mentioned in Henri's journals. However, with only a few exceptions, those people Henri wrote about, eventually paid a heavy price for their illegal activities and greed.
Shortly after NVA forces took over Saigon at the end of April 1975, they began rounding up certain individuals that were on a list. Thanks to Henri Ferrand's six journals that were discovered when the NVA took over the MACV HQ compound, the following people were

also taken into custody:
(1) Khan Le Trang, Minister of the Economy.
(2) General Nguyen Pham Vinh, Prime Minister of South Vietnam.
(3) Brigadier General Tran Van Thien, mayor of Saigon.
(4) Lieutenant General Le Long Quang, former commander of IV Corps in the Mekong Delta.
(5) General Van Nguyen Hoa, former commander of the 25th ARVN Division.
(6) General Duong Pham Diem, former commander of the 5th ARVN Division.
(7) Lieutenant General Tan Pham Huu, President Quoch's security advisor and senior military aide.

Those seven individuals, along with thousands of others, ended up spending the next ten years living in harsh conditions in re-education camps set up by the new Communist government. Everything they owned was confiscated. So, in the end, "the sage of Saigon" helped put away some really bad people after all.

As for President Trung Ho Quoch, his wife, Ly Than Mai, and Vo Tien Dung, President of Air Vietnam, they managed to fly to Hong Kong shortly before NVA T-54 tanks rumbled through the streets of Saigon.

Ngai Bien Phong, South Vietnam's Minister of National Defense and long-time friend of Henri Ferrand, barely made it out of the country. He flew aboard a VNAF helicopter that managed to land safely on an American aircraft carrier in the South China Sea during Operation Frequent Wind, the final evacuation of Americans from the MACV compound and their embassy in downtown Saigon.

Mang Binh Hao and his wife rode out to sea on one of his cargo ships and sailed to Hong Kong. Since he was born Chinese and had lots of money in banks there, it was a natural safehaven for him. His wife, Ling Thi Xuan, the sister of the wife of South Vietnam's president, was even greedier than him though. Two years after establishing a new residence in Hong Kong, she had her husband poisoned so she could inherit his wealth and live a life of luxury with her younger lover.

First Lieutenant Tom Ross was promoted to Captain while still a patient in the psychiatric ward in the 13th Air Force Regional Medical Center at Clark Air Base, Philippines. After several months of treatment for being emotionally and psychologically traumatized for what would later be called PTSD, post-traumatic stress disorder, he was about to be medically discharged "for the good of the service."

Like a boxer in the ring, Ross was only knocked down, not knocked out. He was a true fighter and contacted the former MACV commander and his congressman from Oklahoma. They teamed up to intervene on his behalf. In the end, he was allowed to remain on active duty and was once again assigned to an OSI unit.

Genevieve Ferrand Ross and her uncle, Pierre Ferrand, were buried in a mass grave on the side of Highway 51, along with their fellow travelers, about 40 miles southeast of Saigon. A small sign was erected there to indicate the spot where a bus full of innocent civilians were killed by the Viet Cong on that tragic day in 1972.

The estimated death toll was never 100% accurate because of the condition of the human remains and a lack of records by the bus company. The Viet Cong ended the lives of 32 adults, 4 children and one unborn child that day. That was the real tragic total. The sign with the written estimate was removed in 1975, shortly after the name Saigon was removed from all signs and maps and replaced with Ho Chi Minh City. The Communists didn't stop there though. They renamed all of the roads, streets and boulevards in both Saigon and Cholon as well. They wanted to erase the past but only partially succeeded.

    The seemingly endless war had changed many things, but not the memories of those who survived it or died in it. Some things are, as Genevieve had said, forever.

GLOSSARY

AK-47: Russian-designed Kalashnikov automatic rifle used by the NVA and VC.
ARVN: Army of the Republic of Vietnam.
CO: Commanding officer, usually the highest ranking person in charge.
Civvies: GI slang for civilian clothes.
Lifer: Someone who makes the military a career.
LT: Pronounced "EL TEE," enlisted slang for Lieutenant.
1Lt: First Lieutenant.
MACV SOG: Military Assistance Command Vietnam Studies and Observation Group (aka Special Operations Group), a clandestine organization with tasks that were secretive and not publicized.
NVA: North Vietnamese Army.
VNAF: Vietnamese Air Force.

VIETNAMESE

Bac si: doctor.
Cam on ong: thank you.
Chao ba: "Hello" to a married or elderly woman.
Choi oi: good heavens! or what the hell!
My: Vietnamese word for American.

FRENCH

Bon appetit: good appetite; enjoy your meal.
Bonjour: good day; good morning.
Bon soir: good evening.
C'est la vie: that's life; that's how things happen.
D'accord: agreed; I agree.

GLOSSARY CONT.

Dieu vous garde: God keep you.
Enfant cheri: loved or pampered child.
Merci beau coup: thank you very much/ a lot.
Mon ami: my friend.
Mon cheri: my child.
N'est ce pas?: isn't it so?
Oui: yes.
Sacre bleu: used as a mild oath to express surprise.
S'il vous plait: if you please.
Vive la difference: long live the difference (between the sexes).

ABOUT THE AUTHOR

Steve Crews is the author of SURVIVING BIEN HOA and A DEATH IN KOREA AND THE SEARCH FOR ANSWERS. All of his books can be ordered online at www.trafford.com or email orders@trafford.com. They are also available at major online book retailers.

He was an Air Force "brat" for the first eighteen years of his life before his own twenty-two-year Air Force career began. He is a graduate of Los Angeles City College (Business), Community College of the Air Force (Instructional Technology) and the University of the Philippines (Social Sciences). After a lifetime of traveling in eight countries and all 50 states, he now lives in Mississippi.